FROM TREE TO TABLE

© 2019 by Alan Garbers and Fox Chapel Publishing Company, Inc., 903 Square Street, Mount Joy, PA 17552.

ISBN 978-1-56523-982-1

Library of Congress Cataloging-in-Publication Data

Names: Garbers, Alan, author.
Title: From tree to table / Alan Garbers.
Description: Mount Joy, PA : Fox Chapel Publishing Company, Inc., [2019] | Includes index.
Identifiers: LCCN 2018045954 (print) | LCCN 2018046731 (ebook) | ISBN 9781607656463 (ebook) | ISBN 9781565239821 (softcover)
Subjects: LCSH: Rustic woodwork--Amateurs' manuals. | Furniture making--Amateurs' manuals. | Country furniture--Amateurs' manuals.
Classification: LCC TT195 (ebook) | LCC TT195 .G39 2019 (print) | DDC 684.1--dc23
LC record available at https://lccn.loc.gov/2018045954

To learn more about the other great books from Fox Chapel Publishing, or to find a retailer near you, call toll-free
1-800-457-9112 or visit us at *www.FoxChapelPublishing.com*.

We are always looking for talented authors. To submit an idea, please send a brief inquiry to acquisitions@foxchapelpublishing.com.

Printed in Singapore
First printing

FROM TREE TO TABLE

How to Make Your Own Rustic Log Furniture

ALAN GARBERS

FOX CHAPEL
PUBLISHING

TABLE OF CONTENTS

102

106

110

114

122

126

PART 2: BUILDING THE FURNITURE

128

FOREWORD

My education in the area of making rustic and log furniture came from the College of Hard Knocks. As I was going through each lesson in life, I realized how little information was available about this subject. As I suffered setback after setback, I kept thinking, someone should write a book about this stuff so other folks won't have to endure the pain and suffering I went through. I finally decided I should write this book.

I don't have a fancy studio or gallery, but I have sold and traded my furniture to countless folks across North America. I have even traded my artwork in logs for two free fishing trips in Canada.

Unlike some craftsmen I have encountered, I want to share my experience with you. I want you to succeed and make beautiful furniture. So here it is, from my garage to yours.

Happy building!

INTRODUCTION

Why Rustic and Log Furniture?

There are many reasons why folks love rustic and log furniture.

For some of us, the deep earthy colors of a hickory chair or table is a visual reminder of a family vacation to the wilderness of the Northwoods, of the wild open western United States, of one of the many gorgeous National Park lodges, like those at the Grand Canyon, Yellowstone, or Yosemite. If you paid attention, you'd recognize the familiar basket-weave pattern of hickory used by Old Hickory Furniture. Old Hickory Furniture was manufactured in Martinsville, Indiana, for generations, and Martinsville has been my home for over two decades.

Others may have fallen in love with a piece of locally handcrafted furniture while at a remote hunting or fishing lodge. I think about the clatter of golden aspen leaves in a light breeze while hunting up north when I think about rustic settings. I think of our adventures in the mountains in Arizona, or of bear hunting and muskie fishing in Canada every time I use a piece of aspen.

Some may want to commemorate an old house, shed, or barn from a family homestead by using recycled material from them. For example, I have a bookshelf I made from wood I had been squirreling away from various locations in which we lived over the decades. Some of the wood came from an old shed on a ranch we lived on in Mancos, Colorado. I had used the shed as a blind when hunting for mule deer.

Some of the weathered planks came from an old dump near Hillside, Arizona, that I scavenged from as I drove back and forth from Prescott to a large copper mine in the middle of nowhere.

This bookshelf is a visual compilation of my woodworking life. Pieces of it came from shed, barns, and dumps in Colorado, Arizona, and Indiana. The back is rusted corrugated roofing.

Other boards came from an old shed that I used to make maple syrup in here in Indiana. Along with spending hundreds of hours boiling down syrup, I also learned to play guitar while tending the fire under the evaporator in that shed.

The back is rusted brown corrugated sheet metal from an old hog shed that was tumbling down at another place where we lived, where deer and turkey walked through our yard and coyotes serenaded us at night.

I'd intended to give the bookshelf away, but as I built it, and pulled piece after piece down out of the storage in the rafters, I realized I was making a visual reminder of all the places I had fond memories of. The bookcase was a piece of me, and I of it. I realized I couldn't part with it. The bookcase sits next to me now as I write this.

PART 1

GETTING STARTED

CHAPTER 1
GETTING IDEAS AND FINDING INSPIRATION

For me, getting ideas was never difficult; implementing them has always been the hard part. If you are short on ideas, travel to a state or national park that has a lodge or inn. Almost without exception, they will have log furniture placed in the lobby or other common areas.

Lodges, hotels, and shops are a fantastic place to get ideas for rustic and log furniture. It's a great way to see how other craftsman made their artwork.

I strongly recommend stopping at every rustic and log furniture store you see. Gatlinburg, Tennessee, is almost overrun with log furniture outlets and makers, as are other tourist destinations. Go into any Bass Pro Shop or Cabela's and you'll see countless pieces of log furniture. Take pictures if they allow it. You can't help going away with hundreds of ideas on how to replicate or improve on the furniture you saw.

In some cases, you might think that a piece is too complex to make. It might be, right now. But, as you gain experience (and accrue tools), things that were impossible become possible. In some cases, you might walk away emboldened, thinking, "Heck, I can do better than that!" And you're right, you probably can.

If you still need inspiration, find a copy of *Rustic Artistry for the Home* by Ralph Kylloe. The book is filled cover-to-cover with photos of beautiful log and rustic creations.

Visit living history museums like Cades Cove in Tennessee or Conner Prairie in Indiana. Pioneers made many of their necessities from what was available in the woods and all they had invested was time. The Foxfire series of books documents much of the commonplace knowledge that is fading from society. Among the many topics in the series is making rustic furniture the Appalachian way and even building a lumber kiln.

11

Why Not Buy Log Furniture?

I know why I don't buy every piece of log furniture I fall in love with: I'm not made of money. And, as a woodworker, I always think I can make something like it or better. But, we have bought some items, mainly because there's no way I could build the piece for the price they were asking, nor did I have the time or tools to make it. Let's face it, most of us don't have unlimited space for the ultimate workshop, nor do we have tons of spare time. In some cases, I have to face reality, go against every fiber of my being, and let somebody else do the work for me.

Think Like an Artist but Build Like a Machinist

Log and twigs lend themselves well to whimsical creations. Let your mind flow with the possibilities and reach for the stars. But while doing that, realize things have to hold together and work as desired.

Machinists are very precise. They don't machine anything without a blueprint on how to make it. Every cut and dimension is drawn out long before the mill or lathe is started. A table has to be level. A chair has to sit properly. A coat rack can't fall over when a heavy coat is hung upon it. So, while being creative, also plan it out like a machinist, and make sure it's going to work right before you make the first cut. Start by making a simple drawing of what you want to make. Figure out how tall, wide, and long the piece needs to be to fill the need.

When I say build like a machinist, what I'm saying is to plan the work before cutting, then work the plan while building.

As you read this book, you'll find I repeat myself at times. That's because I know most of you are like me and don't start reading a how-to book at the beginning. We flip through the pages until we find the topic we want to read. So, if I felt one topic was important to know while covering another topic, I went over it again so you won't miss something.

You're welcome.

13

CHAPTER 2
SAFETY FIRST

Chain saw chaps and a hard hat—required PPE for working in the woods. The chaps are made from special fibers that stop a chain saw dead if an accident should happen.

*E*verything about this hobby is dangerous. Life's tough; get a helmet. I'm serious, you should be wearing a hard hat when logging or transporting materials. These days such items are called PPE, which stands for Personal Protective Equipment. PPE is the **minimum** safeguards you need to stay safe. You owe it to your family to put them on each and every time.

Safety in the Woods

Let's think about this. We're using a chain saw that can cut a leg off without even bogging down. The trees we're cutting can weigh enough to crush us like a bug. Trees don't always fall the way we want or act the way we want. Look up as you walk through the woods. Often you'll see broken limbs, dead branches, or heavy vines hanging high above you. One wrong move and they can come crashing down. They don't call them widow-makers for nothing. They don't have to kill you to ruin your day or even your life.

If you're operating a chain saw, you should be wearing chain saw chaps at the very least. Chain saw chaps are made of special fibers that bind a chain saw blade and kill the engine, hopefully before it cuts you. They are cheap insurance.

Wear a hard hat. Remember what I said before? I can't tell you how many times things, large and small, have hit me as I worked in the woods. Every time I wonder, *where in the heck did that come from?* An accident is an accident because you weren't planning on it happening. If you were planning on it, then it would be an "on purpose." That's deep, isn't it? You can mess with fate and wear a hard hat on purpose in case an accident happens.

Wear goggles. You're in the woods, a place filled with swarming bugs that seem attracted to sweat-stained eyes. Let's not forget the branches that somehow find their way to your eye level as you turn your head or stand up. Chain saws throw out wood chips like a beaver on a cocktail of steroids and antidepressants. If you're not wearing eye protection, stuff is going to get in your eyes. Squinting your eyes is *not* protection. Prescription glasses are not going to save you either.

Wear work gloves. Hey, there's a lot of splinters in this line of work, but more importantly, there's also a lot of poison ivy, biting ants, scorpions, spiders, thorns, stickers, fangs, spines, and a zillion other things just waiting to plunge into your flesh if you don't take precautions.

Lastly, wear ear protection. Chain saws are loud enough to cause permanent hearing loss. Do I really need to go into all the reasons why you want to preserve your

Always check around you before cutting trees. Loose branches and widow-makers can ruin your day.

hearing? How about the clatter of aspens, or the whisper of pines, or the bugle of an elk? How about the "I love you" whispered as a child falls to sleep, or your soul mate's intimate desires as you lie close to each other? 'Nuff said.

Safety in the Shop

There isn't a tool made that can't be misused or abused somehow. Woodworking by its very nature is dangerous. We all need to follow safety guidelines.

1. **Keep your tools in good condition.** Dull saws, knives, and chisels force us to apply more force than normal. When something slips, things go bad real quick.

2. **Keep cords in good shape.** The grounding blade is there for a reason, so don't cut it off. Replace frayed or damaged cords.

3. **Keep the floor clean.** Remove any trip hazards or roll hazards. (Sticks and log remnants have a tendency to roll under your feet.) Wet sawdust causes mold.

4. **Beware explosion hazards.** Just about any finish or stain available has a flash point. If you read the label, it most likely says to keep away from open flames. Do I need to remind you that almost all gas water heaters, dryers, stoves, and furnaces have an open flame?

5. **Keep the dust down or eliminated.** Few people realize wood dust is explosive, and a wood shop explosion can blow the doors and windows out of a shop, or even lift the roof. Have a good dust collection system that is properly grounded, or work outside.

6. **Beware of exotic woods.** Some exotic woods cause respiratory issues or contact dermatitis. Even common hardwoods can cause problems. I get a headache after working in an enclosed shop for too long, so I move my gear outside when possible.

7. **Beware knots and defects in the wood.** Knots can come loose or explode when going through a surface planer, or when being cut by a saw. I had one hickory knot explode with such force that it broke blades off the dust fan and blew a hole in the side of the plastic blower housing on my surface planer.

Safety in Your Products

It's a litigation-happy world out there, so don't leave yourself open for a lawsuit by building something dangerous. Years ago, a gallery had a footstool (that someone else made) that used deer antlers as the legs and a cross-section of a log for the seat. It was so top heavy that if someone walked near it, it would fall over, exposing the sharp antler tines like punji sticks. Imagine what would have happened if a child tried to sit on it.

Plan your projects to use materials and fasteners that are appropriate for the task. Plan to have 400-pound (180 kg) people sitting on your benches and chairs. The logs can take it, but can your design or fasteners?

Let's talk about beds. Think of all the activities that happen in a bed. You know what I mean. Can your bed stand up to the rigors of two large people enjoying life? Again, the logs can handle it, but can your design handle the stress?

Your products and artwork have to stand the rigors of normal and abnormal use and abuse without hurting someone.

CHAPTER 3
STYLES OF FURNITURE

N ot all log furniture is the same. Different regions of the country have developed different styles. Almost all of these styles are rooted in the materials available locally.

Northwoods

Much of the furniture found in the North and Northeast rely heavily on birch, and for good reason. Birch has beautiful white bark that can be used as a veneer on furniture. The dark twigs have a distinctive pattern of lenticels that match the lenticel pattern on the birch bark itself.

This Northwoods style of furniture is generally more graceful and complex than other styles. It has been a favorite of furniture lovers for a hundred years or more.

Northwoods-styled furniture is often dominated by birch bark and smaller-diameter wood pieces. The rocker on the left appears to be a more elegant birch and maple combination characteristic of Northwoods pieces.

Midwestern

In the Midwest, hickory is the dominant wood used for furniture. While there are several species of hickory, all have appealing bark patterns that are adored by rustic furniture lovers around the country. Visit just about any lodge in national or state parks and you'll most likely find examples of hickory furniture, some still in use after generations. Old Hickory Furniture in Shelbyville, Indiana, is still producing high-quality pieces to this day.

Hickory dominates pieces that come from the Midwest. The classic bark pattern is very appealing and rugged.

Western

Western log furniture is often made with massive aspen logs, western junipers, and pines. Opposite of the log furniture made in the eastern U.S., western furniture is often oversized, as if to mirror the vastness of the West.

Since the humidity is so low in the western U.S., rot and termites are much less likely to destroy downed wood when compared to the humid eastern U.S. In the arid west, downed wood often dries before damage can set in. As the wood weathers, it takes on a great hue and texture. Artists in the field often use these twisted and weathered wood pieces in their furniture, as well as elk and deer antlers as accents.

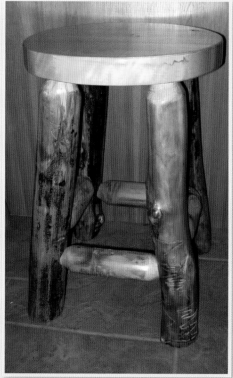

Aspen logs that show signs of insect distress dominate the lodges throughout the western United States. It's easy to see why they're so popular.

19

Southwestern

The furniture history of the Southwest is a rich tapestry. The Spanish colonized parts of Texas, New Mexico, Arizona, and California in the 1500s. The travel route to bring up their belongings from Mexico was more than a thousand miles long over treacherous terrain, so furniture from civilization was limited.

As settlers moved west, they too had little in the way for furniture. At the same time, items that were shipped west were packed in wooden crates and boxes. It was a rare thing that any of the lumber from the crates went unused. It is well documented in journals that crates were pressed into service as almost anything that pioneers needed. Arbuckle's Coffee came in 100-pound (45 kg) crates, which were coveted for their lumber and used for anything from

kitchen cabinets to coffins. In the late 1800s, the majority of coffee sold in Arizona was Arbuckle's brand coffee.

The Sharlot Hall Museum in Prescott, Arizona, has an extensive collection of furniture pieces from the pioneer era. Many of them are made of crate and box lumber.

As dude ranches became popular in the early 1900s, folks scrambled for anything western in style. Furniture often included cattle horns and leather.

These days, Southwestern style encompasses the rich tapestry of the culture and includes elements from the Native American, Spanish, pioneer, and ranching influences. Since the woods found can be so diverse, they often include everything from juniper and ponderosa to creosote and saguaro wood.

CHAPTER 4
LOGS

*L*og and rustic furniture require—Mr. Obvious here—logs. But what logs should you use? It depends on what is available. If you live in Florida, you're not going to have access to western juniper. If you live in Arizona, hickory isn't an option. Your project will have to be made with what is available in your area. I have lived in more states than I care to mention, including the state of confusion. As a result, I have worked with more woods than some of you might have, so I'll share my thoughts.

Finding Logs

Sometimes finding logs is the hardest part. Sure, it may be easy to find logs in general, but what if you want to make a red cedar bed? Or a hickory bed? Or a sassafras bed? Or an aspen bed? You get the idea. And, since most builders want their products to be symmetrical—meaning the legs to be close to the same diameter and shape—it will take more trees than you can imagine to make one bed. If you don't own property with a good selection of trees, you're in trouble.

There are ways to find logs, if you're enterprising:

✓ The first way to find logs is to know someone that has lots of land with a huge selection of trees. Generally, if you ask politely and explain what you're working on, they will allow you to cut a few trees. Now, you might need to resort to a little bribery. In the past, I have been known to offer to make a piece of log furniture in exchange for access to their trees. No one can resist a free table or headboard from trees cut from their own woods. One such trade netted me truckload after truckload of logs.

✓ Some farmers may want their fence line cleared. After all, trees shade crops and reduce their production. The same farmer may want an overgrown pasture thinned. Cows don't eat trees and grass doesn't grow in the shade. Some tree leaves (black cherry) can actually poison livestock. Be sure to pile all the "slash" neatly and out of the way. (Slash is logger talk for the branches and undesirable cuts of wood nobody wants.)

✓ Anyone that has a tree farm has a running battle of TSI. That's forester talk for Timber Stand Improvement. If someone is managing their forest for valuable hardwoods, they need to remove the undesirable trees regularly so that the valuable saplings and young trees get plenty of sunlight and nutrients. It is a hard job and rarely ever as complete as it should be. Fast-growing trees like sassafras, locust, yellowwood, and other species can quickly outpace a white oak, walnut, or black cherry. If left to grow wild, the more valuable but slower-growing trees will get shaded out and die off, leaving a thick stand of junk wood. Work with a forester or landowner to perform TSI and you will get more logs than you can ever use. Just remember to not drive over, walk on, or drop trees on the valuable trees. The good thing is that you usually don't need to do anything with

Crowded woods cause trees to rapidly reach for the sun, resulting in saplings that are perfect for furniture.

the slash. The idea is to let nature do its thing and put the nutrients back into the ground as the slash rots. Another positive is that the slash provides good cover for birds and animals hiding from predators.

✓ Often, state and federal forest managers offer a firewood-cutting permit or fence post permit. For a small fee the rules are fairly simple; cut your wood in a specified area directed by the manager or don't cut more than your permit allows.

✓ Speaking of fence posts, sometimes farmers and ranchers want to clear out or replace old fences. In many cases, they use a bulldozer to shove the posts and fence wire into a huge pile. It can take some sweat and hard work to separate them, but some of those old posts are beautifully weathered with decades of distressing that gives each one unique character.

✓ Some homeowners want trees thinned or removed from their yard. Unless the trees are small and manageable, I would stay away from such things because it doesn't take much to drop a tree in an unexpected direction and flatten a car or house.

Advertising on social media or community sites is a great way to get the word out that you're looking for logs. Even if you don't get enough logs to finish a project, keep the logs and set them aside for a later date when you have access to more.

The Art of Coppicing

Here's one more thing to think about. Many hardwoods start new growth once the tree is cut down. This new growth spurts up fast because it has a mature root system supporting it. Tulip poplar, maple, ash, oak, willow, alder, and sassafras often send up a dozen or more new shoots off a cut stump. It doesn't take long before you have a new crop of sapling wood to use.

While this may be a shock to folks in the U.S., it's an ancient practice in Europe called coppicing. The practice is a fast way to grow fence material, roof thatching, firewood, and, for us, furniture material.

Generally speaking, it is best to cut the tree in the dormant stage of winter. Cut the tree close to the ground and then let nature do its thing. By the next fall, there can be suckers with five feet (1.5 m) of new growth.

Man isn't the only one that makes use of coppiced trees. Deer love the new tender shoots as they grow, especially those of sassafras trees. I've seen browsing on new growth that was caused by deer that looked like a madman with a machete had been at work on it.

This tulip poplar was cut ten years ago. Since then a number of new saplings have sprung up, all the perfect size for furniture.

This stump was cut a year before. It won't take long before these suckers are ready to use for projects.

Cutting the Wood in the Right Season

These days, when you buy firewood or lumber, it is often labeled "seasoned," implying it has dried for a season. Historian, artist, and writer Eric Sloane had another theory. "Seasoned" wood was wood that our ancestors *cut in the right season*. That's what *we* need to do. Our logs need to be cut in the right season or our lives get incredibly difficult. To understand what I'm talking about we need to understand the seasons of a tree.

Contrary to what most folks think, the sap does not go "down" into the roots in the fall and "up" into the tree in the summer. With that being said, some trees do have copious flows of "sap" during the growing season, maples being the most famous. However, there are certain times of the year when the moisture content in the tree diminishes.

As the seasonal dry spell in late summer withers your garden, so does it dry out trees. The poor things are working hard to extract water from the ground to replenish the water lost in the leaves. Some trees can expel 200 gallons (750 liters) of water a day! This dry period can be stressful for the trees, and some may drop their leaves early to save themselves.

During this season, the moisture content in the tree drops to about the lowest point all year. I don't take advantage of this time because I don't like working in the heat and I don't want to chance that the tree wasn't finished with that chemical process of growing that makes the bark slip (more on this later in the book).

As the fall rains and early winter snows come, the moisture content increases again, then it falls in mid-winter. Old-timers will tell you that this is the best season to cut wood, relating back to what Eric Sloane said about "seasoned" wood. I tested this with a moisture indicator and it seems to be true. During a cold spell in February, I cut a supply of sassafras logs. The sapwood close to the bark had 29–31%, while the heartwood measured 19–20% MC.

Why should you be concerned about moisture content (MC)? Two reasons: wood movement, and rot. As wood dries, it shrinks, splits, twists, and bends. Using whole logs cuts down on much of this, but you still have to think about it.

Due to my inexperience, this beautiful bed was destroyed by rot, all because I didn't let the wood dry properly.

Rot is the biggest problem. If you cut logs with the intent to keep the bark on, you want the MC to be as low as possible. Anything above 20% and rot can form, bark can slip, and insects run amok. If you imprudently use wet wood and then coat it with a finish, you lock in the water and it can never escape.

Case in point: I foolishly made a bed from hornbeam birch with the bark on. I had cut the logs only six months earlier. I did not have a moisture meter at the time and I assumed the wood was dry enough.

The rippling muscle look of the bed logs was beautiful after I gave it two coats of polyurethane. What made this bed really special was that each spindle in the headboard was a white-tail deer buck rub! (For you non-hunters and naturalists, bucks rub small trees with their antlers to mark their territory and to rub the velvet off their antlers.)

To make a long story not so long, I had big plans of selling this very unique bed for huge bucks (get it…that's a play on words). I set the bed sections aside and went to work on my next masterpiece. The months slipped away and I never had a chance to market the bed, which was a good thing.

Almost a year after I cut the logs, I pulled the bed out of the shadows to get it ready to sell at Christmas. To my horror, there was mold growing *under* the finish, blistering it. I checked the moisture content with my newly acquired moisture meter, only to find it was still 31−33% MC!

By this time, my experience had grown to where I had built a small wood kiln that heated and dehumidified the wood. I took the sections and placed them in it and tried to dry them out for a few weeks. No deal. With the polyurethane encasing the bark, the logs became miniature saunas. When I pulled them out, they were black with mold! Talk about devastated. I could have cried as I dismantled the bed and burned most of it.

So, after totally confusing you, here's the simple version: **Spring and summer**—This is the season where the tree grows larger, both in height and girth. The sap flows heavily as the tree adds new wood just under the bark. During this time, the bark is loose, like a sock on your foot. Relatively speaking, this is the easiest time of year to peel the bark off. I say *relatively* because some trees are easier to peel than others.

Fall and winter—This is the dormant season. The bark is stuck on like glue and will not come off without a great deal of work. Even when it does come off, a great deal of damage is done to the wood underneath.

Plan accordingly for the type of logs you want for your furniture.

Where to Find the Best Trees

Unless you live in a house built by Dr. Seuss, your house is built with right angles; walls are straight and the same thickness at the top as they are at the bottom. Dimensional lumber is made to maintain a uniform size and thickness from stud to stud, joist to joist, rafter to rafter. This makes it much easier to build a house that is square and trim. Drywall fits correctly, trim fits correctly, etc.

The problem with logs is that none of them are the same size from top to bottom. Oh, some of them look like it, but despite their looks, the log is smaller on top than it is on the bottom. This makes getting our dimensions right during the build difficult. The top rail of a headboard needs to be slightly longer than the bottom rail, and other little things like that. So, the closer the logs are to milled lumber, or perfectly symmetrical columns, the easier it is for us to use in our projects.

The big question is "Where do we find the straightest logs in the forest?" That's easy. Go to where the woods are the thickest. Foresters call it Early Successional Growth (ESG). In reality, we want the mid to later stages of ESG. Here's why: A tree is trying to grab as much sunlight as possible so it can do its thing and grow. If you notice as you drive around the countryside, yard trees with no trees around them are very bushy with lots of branches, but generally no towering main trunks. There might only be one tree per acre. They don't need to grow tall to find sunlight. To make matters worse, often the trunk is more pyramid shaped than column-shaped.

In a thick part of the woods, the trees are competing for the sunlight. Starting out after a farm field turns fallow, a forest is logged, or a forest fire rages through, there might be 20,000 saplings per acre. In their battle for the sunlight, the trees keep racing upward to beat the other trees for sunlight. In the process, the lower branches stop receiving sunlight and die. Eventually, they rot away or break off. This process often makes trees as straight and columnlike as we are ever going to find in nature. For the most part, those are the trees we want for our furniture.

A fallow field quickly reverts back to forest. I cut dozens of ash saplings from this stand, all straight as an arrow.

TREES TO AVOID

I feel I should caution you about trees you shouldn't cut.

- **Never cut trees that the property owner wants to keep.** It's money out of their pocket if you do.

- **Never cut trees that may fall on valuable trees.** Loggers are experts on dropping trees in directions away from valuable trees, but unless you're experienced in the matter, don't risk it. One wrong cut can cost the property owner thousands of dollars in destroyed timber.

- **Beware trees that are holding up a "widow-maker."** The weight of a dead branch or even an entire tree pushing against the tree you want to cut can create a huge hazard. Often, there is no warning that a branch or dead tree is falling until it's already too late.

- **Beware a leaning tree.** There are two distinct hazards of cutting a leaning tree:

  - If the cut is made from the side it is leaning toward, the weight can cause the tree to lean more, pinching the saw blade. In many cases, another saw has to be used to complete the cut from the opposite side. The extra pressure and a twisting tree can damage a saw blade.

  - If the cut is made from the side opposite the direction of lean, as the cut is made, the weight is often too much for the remaining fibers to hold. The tree splits, often without warning. This violently thrusts the loose section of the tree trunk back toward the cutter. This can have unbelievable springlike energy that can impale anyone in the way. Loggers call the remaining tree stump a "barber's chair."

- **Beware a yard tree.** Many yard trees have been the home for tree houses, swings, and who-knows-what. Yard trees are often riddled with buried nails and other bits of metal. All it takes is one nail to ruin a band saw or chain saw blade.

- **Beware a fence line tree.** Like a yard tree, they can have wire fencing and staples buried in them. But, usually, the tree is clear above the four-foot (1.2 m) line.

- **Blistering, rotten, or otherwise damaged trees should be avoided.** Sassafras trees rot and blister even as they grow. If you live in the humid areas of the U.S., be wary of any wood on the ground. I would quarantine any suspect wood in a sunny and dry area until it is proven clean. Rotten wood has no place in furniture. The last thing you want is to bring termites into your shop.

Selecting Trees

Starting out, select trees that are as straight as can be found. The straighter and more cylindrical a log is, the easier it is to work with. It will make designing and building furniture much easier. As you gain skill and experience, you can use less-perfect logs that will give your furniture wonderful character.

I often start off into the woods with a project in mind and I want to see if I can find the wood to support the idea. I usually carry bright surveyor's ribbon to mark the trees I think I want. That makes it much easier to find the right trees when I return with a saw.

While selecting trees, we need to realize what size of logs we need for the project. Two-inch-diameter (50 mm) logs work great for bar stools. Four- to six-inch (100–150 mm)

logs are about right for bedposts. Three-inch (75 mm) logs work well for crosspieces on a headboard. Small saplings of various sizes work well for braces and decorative members.

Bear in mind that humans like symmetrical things. We like to see things that match in color and size. A bar stool with varying sizes of legs is going to look awkward, and a set of them is going to be even worse. My point? Be sure to cut enough wood of matching size to do the project. In fact, cut extra wood. Why? Because it takes a long time for wood to dry, and running out of wood can delay a project for a year or more.

I made a mistake years ago. A lodge owner wanted me to make a set of bar stools, but he wanted to see one first before he committed to the deal. I went to work and made one heck of a bar stool, which included a forked hickory stick in the backrest. It was my way of showing off what I could do and a way to use up something I had been saving for that "special" project. Dang it if the lodge owner didn't love the bar stool and wanted all of them to have forked sticks in the back! Do you know how hard it was to find three more forked hickory sticks of the same size for the backs? Do you know how hard it was to get the sticks dry and on the stools in the allotted time? I learned my lesson.

I can't say this enough: Cut lots of extra wood. Some trees are very prone to rot that can't be seen from outside; sassafras is notorious for this.

Avoid heavy branching. Trees that grow in the open are notorious for this. Each branch is a knot you have to deal with. If you insist upon using a tree with lots of branches,

cut and peel it in the early summer so the bark will be easier to remove around the branches.

Another issue is bark or wood coloration. Again, sassafras can be a nightmare for color differences. Sassafras is a wood that looks best with the bark on but sanded to reveal the redwood-colored bark underneath the weathered bark. The color variation can be maddening, but somewhat predictable if attention is paid to how old the tree is. Young, fast-growing trees have a lighter, yellowish red bark without much in the way of vulgs. Older trees have a bold, beautiful red with moderate vulgs. Old trees have a deep, dark red with deep vulgs. In case you're wondering, vulgs are the deep splits that are made in the bark as the tree grows.

The last thing you want to happen is to run out of wood. Your projects will suffer for it.

Hardwoods vs. Softwoods

Trees are divided into two classes: hardwoods and softwoods.

Basically, hardwoods are any trees with a leaf, and softwoods are any trees with a needle. So, ash, oak, and aspen are hardwoods, while pines and cedars are softwoods. But don't assume any hardwood is going to have hard wood. Cottonwood, poplar, and aspen are all hardwoods, but their wood can be very soft and easy to cut, break, or damage.

On the opposite end of the scale, dogwood, hickory, oak, and some types of birch can be extremely hard. Ironwood, an understory type of birch, was used for wooden mallets. Hickory is still used for tool handles and

ash is still used for baseball bats. Some types of oaks were used for warships in sailing days.

Softwoods are softer woods and very easy to work with. But, compared to woods such as ash and oak, softwoods are structurally weaker when compared size for size.

When it comes to making chair seats and bed rails— the part that holds up the mattress—I prefer to use clear oak. Why clear? Large defects or knots that would look great as a tabletop are weaknesses in the wood. In some cases, using such a piece as a structural member, meaning one that will hold weight, could lead to a broken piece of furniture and an angry end user.

CHAPTER 5
PEELING BARK

*Q*uite often, when the subject of log furniture is brought up, the conversation leads to a drawknife and cutting bark off logs. If someone tells you that, just smile, because I'm going to tell you a secret that will keep the back-breaking chore of using a drawknife to an absolute minimum. That's not to say I don't have and use a drawknife, but we'll save that for another section.

If you want wood that will be used bark-off, bide your time until the spring. In the seasonal cycle of trees, spring is the time that trees are working to produce a new layer of wood. This occurs from April to early June in the Midwest. During this process, the tree adds new wood just under the bark. During the growing process, the bark is basically floating on the new wet growth. Cut the tree down and the bark comes off almost as easy as pulling off a sock.

Peeling Bark the Easy Way

Avoid using sharp things to help it. Leave the drawknife in the drawer. In fact, leave all the sharp things in the toolbox. All that is needed is a dull screwdriver and a putty knife, preferably well used with rounded corners. Wood has a wonderful natural texture to it as is. If a sharp tool is used to pry the bark off, those marks will mar the surface and show very distinctly when it dries.

To remove the bark, first work the screwdriver under the bark at the cut edge. It will separate fairly easily, some woods easier than others. Once it's started, use the putty knife to slit the bark and pry it up. Use your fingers as much as possible. (Wear gloves.) Once started, the tools can usually be set aside and the bark can be pulled off in strips by hand.

I generally throw the bark strips away, but I imagine crafty people could use them for other projects, such as edge strips and weavings.

A word of caution: Wasps and hornets seem to love the juices that are found under the bark and will ruin your day if you're not careful. I recommend tossing the bark strips off to the side so that you're not accidentally stomping on mad flying insects that can sting.

When saplings are cut in the spring and early summer, the bark often peels off easily.

29

Bark strips are very strong and could be used to weave baskets and chair seats.

Saving Bark

Bark itself is a valuable item. It can be used as a veneer over a plywood base to make beautiful furniture. Lovely white paper birch bark is a classic for Northwoods crafts. Here in Indiana, yellowwood bark is very beautiful and easy to procure. Many foresters want the yellowwood trees killed during TSI sessions. Double-ringing them and removing the bark is a surefire way to do so. The problem is that the bark wants to curl back up as it dries. Sections of bark need to be clamped down to prevent curling. But the bark is also very wet and has a tendency to mold. Mold has a harder time growing in moving air, so I use a box fan to keep the air moving as I dry it.

Bark from trees such as hickory and white oak often break off naturally. They can be used for accents on furniture.

Bark from a tulip poplar can be very pretty. If cut at the right time, the bark comes off in perfect sheets. Only do this to trees that you want to kill in TSI.

Peeling Bark the Hard Way

I know I have repeatedly told you to avoid using a drawknife—and for good reason—but a drawknife *is* required to achieve certain looks. Most importantly, it gives the logs a true hand-hewn appearance. Folks pay large sums of cash for hand-hewn flooring and ceiling beams. It makes sense to cash in on some of that money. Plus, if I didn't include how to use a drawknife, it might look like I don't know how to make real log furniture!

✓ TIP
Before using a drawknife on any wood, I recommend using an aggressive sanding wheel mounted on a right-angle grinder to smooth all of the knots. Preparing the log in this manner makes peeling it much easier and cleaner.

31

Using a drawknife is hard work and makes a huge mess, but it is required on some pieces.

Logs have two layers of bark, as outlined by the red and black lines. Clean peeling requires removing both. Skip peeling requires removing all of the outer layer and most of the inner layer.

✓ TIP
Fresh green wood peels much easier than dried wood.

There are three basic looks that require a drawknife.

Clean peel
The most common look is a clean peel. This refers to the fact that all inner and outer bark has been removed, leaving the wood clean. Even with a clean peel, there are often discolorations in the wood that are appealing. Unless the cut marks are sanded away, it is obvious that the log has been peeled with a drawknife. This look appeals to many people, as it reminds them of the "olden days."

A clean peel is exactly what it sounds like; all bark has been removed.

Skip peel

As the name suggests, portions of the log are skipped. This doesn't mean you should leave the thick outer bark. The skip peel refers to leaving strips of the inner bark. The inner bark is very light in most cases but often dries darker. It will take some experience to get the exact look you desire. Using a skip peel technique highlights the fact that the log has been hand peeled with a tool. In my opinion, a light skip peel is the most attractive look when using a drawknife.

Scraped bark

Some bark, such as pine, produces a scaly appearance as if corn flake cereal was glued on the surface. Scraping the bark with the dull edge of a putty knife or dragging a drawknife backward knocks the loose scales off. Lightly sanding the bark afterward can smooth away rough spots.

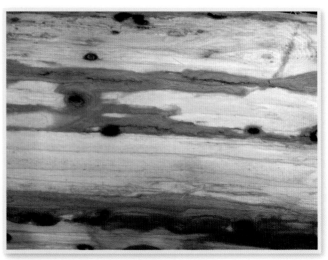

The bark remnants left after a skip peel accent the drawknife cuts.

Black cherry bark is very scaly and looks similar to many softwoods, such as pine.

Scraping the loose bark off and sanding the surface smooth provides a unique look for furniture.

When nature lends a hand

Sometimes a tree dies and dries standing upright. This happens in the arid western states more so than in the humid eastern United States. As the tree dries, insects, wind, and rain slowly strip the bark away, leaving a rare, weathered wood patina that is impossible to replicate with tools. Old juniper fence posts that are common from the Great Plains to the Pacific Ocean have a similar look. It might take some time and looking to find enough suitable matching wood to make a piece of furniture, but the beauty it radiates is worth the extra time and work.

The fresh-peeled tulip poplar (bottom) is visually boring when compared to the patina and character of weathered cedar (top).

CHAPTER 6
WHY WOOD SHRINKS, WARPS, AND CRACKS

*P*rior to the industrial age, woodworkers had to work with wood instead of forcing wood to work for them. What do I mean by that? Most wood products these days are supplemented with super-strong epoxy, compressed for added strength, engineered out of wood chips, treated with chemicals, and covered with sheets of plastic. These products don't rely on the natural strengths of wood; they rely on technology.

Sassafras has a tendency to check as it dries. It doesn't affect the strength of the log, and some find it appealing.

Learning from Our Ancestors

Before men had machines and technological advancements to do most of the work, craftsmen had to be frugal and minimize wasted effort and learned how to work with the wood to make the best product. They knew cutting wood in the right season meant less drying time. They knew cutting wood in a quartersawn fashion meant less warping and twisting. They could read the natural stresses in wood and use them to their advantage to make a strong product. They knew which woods worked best for specific tasks, whether it was to carve a gunstock, make a mallet, make a door, or build a ship.

A good example would be the use of southern live oaks that had massive branching close to the trunk. The natural arch that resulted was extremely strong when used as knee bracing in sailing ships. It was a brace made by the force of nature that few if any craftsman today would even think of.

Our ancestors knew how to use or eliminate the natural stresses found in wood. As you work with wood, you too will learn how to deal with them and use them to your advantage. As I recommended before, the Foxfire series of books covers much of this information, as did Eric Sloane.

Checking

No, checking isn't writing bank drafts to pay your bills. Checking is the natural splitting of the log as it dries. Logs split because the exterior of the log dries sooner than the interior of the log. As the wood cells dry, they shrink. Sometimes the stress of shrinking causes the wood cells to pull apart. A crack starts. This allows the drying process to speed up in that location, which causes even more shrinkage, which causes even more stress and more checking.

We can try to prevent or lessen it by coating the ends of the log with wax or anchor seal, but why bother? In most cases, **checking has little to no effect on the strength of the log.** Plus, I have had buyers tell me how much they love the look of the split logs. They say it looks rustic. They buy the furniture, so who am I to say they're wrong?

This walnut table has severe checking that only adds to its beauty.

Warping

If you've worked with wood at all, you've dealt with warped wood. Warping is caused by stresses induced by uneven drying, or by uneven wetting. Warping isn't a huge problem in logs, but it can be on boards. Warping can be minimized by quartersawing the log when cutting lumber.

It is very time consuming and wastes some wood, but having unusable lumber is also a huge waste.

If a board has a simple belly-type warp, try laying the belly of the wood on a damp towel. Monitor the board.

The wood should start to arch away from the towel. When it is flat, set it aside to dry.

While I stated that logs don't usually suffer from warping, there is an exception. In my experience logs that are naturally bent bend even more as they dry.

Cracking

Logs often crack at the ends as they dry. In most cases, the cracks don't travel far and can be eliminated by trimming the log after it's dry.

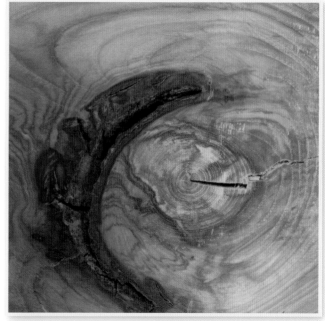

Small cracks have no effect on a log.

Loose Bark

Some woods are prone to losing bark, especially when insects find their way to the tasty new wood that was formed just under the bark. If a small section pops off, glue can fasten it right back on. If I suspect that a piece of bark at the end cut of a log might come loose, I set it upright and allow CA glue to fill the crack. If everything works right, the bark should be on for good once the glue dries. Just be aware that CA can take days to dry if it isn't exposed to the air.

Knots and Voids

As you build furniture, keep in mind that knots add very little in the way of strength. If the knot or even a void in the wood is in the center of a board, it most likely won't affect the strength of the board. But a knot on the edge of a board is a weak spot and can greatly diminish its load capacity. While you most likely won't have to worry about such things when building furniture, bear it in mind if the piece needs to support a great deal of weight, such as with a bed frame or chair leg.

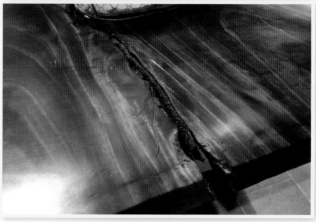

Voids may lessen the strength of a piece and create a place for dust, dirt, and grime to build up. Tinted epoxy can fill the voids.

35

The Magic of 20 Percent

The first goal is to get the wood to less than twenty percent moisture content. As stated before, wood is food to many things: carpenter ants, termites, ambrosia beetles, mold, and other things that love to live in and on wood. But they rely on the moisture in the wood to live. As the moisture content drops, so do the problems associated with the pests.

Twenty percent moisture content is the magic number, below which mold and most pests can't live. So how do we check moisture content? The market is filled with expensive and cheap moisture meters. Woodworkers aren't the only people concerned about moisture content. Grain storage facilities, ethanol plants, medicine producers, and countless others require accurate moisture readings. The more accurate the readings need to be, the more costly the metering device becomes. Luckily, we don't need to be that accurate, so an inexpensive digital meter is close enough.

Most meters have two metal pins that are lightly jabbed into the wood. The more moisture that's in the wood, the more current can flow. The meter does the math and you have a reading of moisture content in big, bold numbers.

A word of caution: Some cheap meters don't display a number above the thirty percent range. That doesn't mean it's broken; it just means that the moisture content is above the scale it is calibrated for. So if you take periodic readings with such a meter, don't expect to see a change for quite some time.

The next number you're shooting for is what's stable in your area. Believe it or not, your house and furniture are constantly absorbing and expelling moisture, depending on the humidity and temperature. In the summer, the humidity goes up. In the winter, it goes down. Homes that are air-conditioned (heated and cooled) have minimal changes. Areas that are not air-conditioned can have wide fluctuations in humidity.

Our goal is to get the wood to a point that is close to the moisture content of the place in which it is going to be used. For me, it's about seven percent content. How do you find this number in your area? Use the meter on an exposed building member, like a stud, wood trim, etc.

A moisture meter (left) is a valuable tool when drying wood. A metal detector (right) is required to find nails and screws before running reclaimed wood through woodworking equipment.

Why is this important? As wood absorbs or expels moisture, it expands and contracts. If we use wood that is too moist, the joint will loosen as it dries. If we use wood that is too dry, it can swell and split tenon joints or buckle tabletops. (Rarely is your wood going to be too dry.)

Another key reason to allow the wood to fully dry is stability. As wood dries, parts of the same board are going to shrink more in one direction than another. Depending on how the tree grew, shrinkage rates can vary in the same direction, just inches apart.

Imagine making beef jerky. Does the jerky ever look like the cut of meat it started out as? In case you've never made jerky, the answer is no. The meat shrinks, twists, and curls depending on how lean it was and which way the grain was. Wood is no different. We want all that movement to be done before we start working with it. If we don't, we may be doing a lot of work for nothing.

When I first started, I decided to make a beautiful cedar log bed. I even made the side rails that held the mattress out of two logs each. The bed looked fantastic and I was already counting the money I was going to sell it for. But, not having a buyer interested, I set the bed pieces aside, unassembled.

Months later, I decided to take it to a shop to sell. But, because life hates me, the side rail tenons on one side wouldn't line up with the holes bored into the headboard. Try as I may, using every trick I could think of, I could not force the tenon into the hole. All my work was wasted. I had to redo the entire side rail. I had just completed another class in the college of hard knocks.

Any logs left in the weather start to rot. These logs might be too far gone and have become "punky." The best thing to do is remove the bark with a drawknife and check the wood underneath. With luck, the wood will be solid but spalted.

CHAPTER 7
FOUND WOOD

This is a rustic find at its best. These harness hooks were made from branches cut from log sections.

*F*ound wood is just another term for recycled wood or repurposed wood. You can find "found wood" anywhere. I'm sure you've seen crafts made from pallets. Using pallets isn't new. Ingenious folks have been using found wood for as long as man has been cutting it up. Prior to the use of cardboard, almost everything came packed in wooden crates. These crates found their way into kitchen cabinets, pie coolers, bed slats, china hutches, and anything else that was needed. So, in the tradition of the pioneers, don't overlook pallets, crates, or shipping skids, for two reasons.

First, they're authentic material for rustic furniture. If you ever get to Sharlot Hall Museum in Prescott, Arizona, you'll see furniture made from crates. If you read the journals and biographies of trading post operators, you see that the shipping crates they received were almost as valuable as the items that came packed in them.

Second, you may find some valuable wood. A prime example is when exotic woods come in from South America. I watched time after time as freighters would offload bundles of rough-cut mahogany planks for the furniture market. As they stacked the bundles, they used four-inch square (100 x 100 mm) planks, known as sleepers, to leave a gap for the fork truck to pick up the wood. Those sleepers were also prime mahogany. As the wood was loaded onto trucks and shipped, guess what was left as garbage all over the pier? You guessed it, hundreds of mahogany sleepers that made great woodworking projects.

Another example comes from right here in the heartland of the USA. Indiana is ground zero for the worldwide hardwood industry. Walnut, white oak, black cherry, and other valuable hardwood trees are cut and shipped daily. Along with the valuable lumber are the logs that don't make the cut, so to speak. Many of those logs make it into the pallet market. So, while many pallets are made of low-quality beech or pine, they also might be made of low-grade hardwoods. But what makes them low-grade? Good question.

Hardwood buyers want clear, defect-free, veneer-grade wood. They don't want anything with knots, burls, spalting, crotches, or things of that nature. Those pieces get made into pallets. But those defects are the very things that make wood interesting to look at and therefore are prime pieces for rustic furniture.

Old lumber from these authentic Arbuckle coffee crates were used extensively in the Old West.

Running reclaimed native lumber though a surface planer accents saw cuts and nail holes beautifully.

39

Older homes were often made of native lumber, native meaning that it came from local sources. In the Midwest, native lumber is often valuable hardwoods. In years past, farmers would clear land and make timbers out of the trees they cleared. I have heard stories of barns being built of black walnut beams. In my own home, I have found black walnut boards being used as a coal bunker in the basement. Some of the pieces made their way into a hall table I made. A friend has a house with white oak car siding interior walls in the living room! A close inspection of the boards revealed that the wood was originally damaged by insects. This probably caused the sawmill to sell it for low-grade lumber. Ironically, if the right buyer saw the distressed boards now, they would give a small fortune for them. Many upscale log home builders scout the countryside searching for old wood to make into beautiful distressed flooring.

A word of warning: Before you get too attached to old wood, consider the age. Prior to 1978, many paints were made with lead. Sanding or running the painted wood through a jointer or planer would put lead-impregnated dust into the air. Lead-paint chips can also fall off items made with it. If in doubt, don't use it.

Other places to find "found wood" are river floodplains, lake shores, river banks, old sheds, old barns, dumps, etc. But before you go hog wild and rip down or collect something, remember that buildings and dumps that have historical interest, such as ghost towns, old mines, etc., may be protected by law. You can't afford the fines, the jail time, or the hate mail if you remove a cherished landmark. If you don't own it, get permission from the owner before taking a crowbar to it.

Another point: Before you start picking through a logjam in a river for the perfect piece of wood, check the laws governing it. People have gotten fined for removing what they considered a hazard to water navigation, only to find out the state considered it valuable fish habitat when the water was back up to normal pool (level).

One last point: Critters that sting, bite, slither, and crawl love to live in old piles of tin and lumber. Take extra caution when dealing with such things. Fire ants, rattlesnakes, black widow spiders, wasps, brown recluse spiders, hornets, carpenter bees, African killer bees, and other nasty things are no fun.

Barnwood is highly sought after, once it's cleaned.

Old galvanized roofing complements rustic furniture. It was used here as the back to a barn wood bookcase.

Steel Roofing

Think back to the times you have been at a cabin in the woods. Quite often the roof on the cabin is galvanized steel corrugated panels. Over the years the tin wears off and turns a rusty brown. When they get replaced, the old roofing is often sold to a scrap dealer for the going rate of junk steel. That's a shame because many rustic designers use that worn roofing as paneling in rustic-flavored restaurants and shops. You can also use the old roofing as backs to hutches, bookshelves, headboards, and more. The result can be quite beautiful.

The only caution is to make sure all sharp edges are covered in a manner that keeps people from being cut.

Buyers are not going to be happy if they have to renew their tetanus shot because of your furniture.

If you don't want to risk snakes, hornets, and tetanus shots, you can make your own rustic steel roofing. Almost any home store has the corrugated roofing for sale. Wiping it down with vinegar will dull the shiny surface. Use heavy grit sandpaper to scratch through the galvanized surface in places. Giving it a bath of salty water will speed up the rust process. The roofing doesn't have to be totally rusted, just enough to knock off the newness.

Yard sales and flea markets are a great place to find components for furniture. This iron table stand was just a few dollars.

Other Found Materials

As you stroll through flea markets, yard sales, and, yes, even dumps, keep an eye out for old hardware, door knobs, locks, and other rustic items that might make a cool focal point on a piece of furniture. Also, be on the lookout for furniture, or parts of furniture, that can be repurposed. As an example, I found a wrought-iron table base at a yard sale. The base already looked rustic and cool. All I had to add was a top that set it off.

CHAPTER 8
BARK ON OR BARK OFF?

Woods can be divided into bark on and bark off. Some woods have a special look that, as an artist, you will want to make the most of. Some woods look best with the bark on. Sassafras, hickory, and hornbeam birch are just a few that look great with the bark on. Cedar, ash, maple, and pine look better with the bark off.

Bark-On Wood

Sassafras

This fast-growing tree has *roots* deep in our history. Sassafras has a distinct root beer smell, and in fact its roots were used to make root beer. The roots were also thought to "cure" everything from gout to rheumatism, so much so that the king of England made it the law that every man in Jamestown had to provide sassafras roots as a tax. Some folks also felt that sassafras wood warded off evil. Cribs, bible boxes, spoons, and other things were made from sassafras. Had Linda Blair slept in a sassafras log bed in the movie *Exorcist*, she would have been safe. End of movie.

Sassafras loves to twist and turn and make great shapes. Its bark turns bright red when sanded. It looks great and grows fast, just what you want in a tree.

Sassafras in its natural state is a dull wood to look at. But, if the outer surface of bark is taken off with a rasp or sander, it exposes a beautiful red inner bark.

The downside? Sassafras rots fast, often while still on the stump. One part of the tree will be fine and sound, three feet further it can be as rotten as Captain Hook's heart. So, cut twice as much as you need, during winter, and don't let it lay on the ground.

Hickory

You have to love hickory. It grows straight as an arrow, sometimes has a cool basket weave pattern in the bark, is strong, and is mostly rot free. Sand the bark and you get a warm brown color. Hickory is a favorite of professional log furniture makers, including the world-famous Old Hickory Furniture here in Indiana. If you've seen old log furniture in the lodges of our national parks, chances are it came from Old Hickory.

Hickory has a wonderful basket weave pattern to the bark. With a little sanding or staining, it can become a warm brown that is recognized across the country.

44

There's a reason for its popularity. No commercially harvested wood is stronger than hickory. The dense wood is legendary in its ability to take abuse and resist shock.

✓ Some Native American dialects refer to hickory as the "bow" tree, as it was and still is favored for self bows.

✓ Pioneers used the dense wood for anything that needed to stand up to repeated abuse. Wagon wheel spokes, ladder rungs, flooring, and tool handles are all still made from hickory.

✓ Initially, baseball bats used hickory before the industry turned to ash. In recent decades a few companies are returning to the use of hickory for bats.

✓ President Andrew Jackson was called "Old Hickory" because of his strong, unwavering leadership traits.

✓ Even the bark stands up to abuse. While other types of trees are prone to have their bark pop off when hit, hickory bark holds up to it for generations.

The point is, hickory is a great wood to use for furniture.

Because of its characteristics, hickory furniture components can be smaller, giving the piece a more refined and elegant look when compared to some of the bulkier aspen and pine furniture.

Hickory also lends itself well to steam bending.

Because of its density, hickory is also very hard on tools. Saws, planer knives, and sandpaper quickly wear out when used on hickory. While this raises the cost to process hickory, it is an investment because well-made hickory furniture sells.

Hickory also quickly and readily regrows when coppiced. It is nature's gift that keeps on giving.

Hornbeam birch

Also known as muscle beech and ironwood, this unique understory tree is strong, hard, and grows like a rippling muscle. Its bark is a grayish green, which accents the muscle look. Anything you make with hornbeam will turn heads. The cool thing is it fits right in on California's Muscle Beach. (Get it . . . muscle beech . . . Muscle Beach . . .) The bad thing about hornbeam birch is that the bark tends to pull away from the wood as it dries. You may need to cut double to triple the normal amount of wood just to get a project done.

Hornbeam Birch has interesting musclelike ripples. For some reason, whitetail bucks also love to use them as rubs to mark their territory.

Bark-Off Wood

Any wood can be a bark-off wood, but here are few that I have worked with:

Ash

Heavy and strong, ash will stand up to anything you throw at it (which is why it is used for baseball bats). Ash grows like a weed in moist areas, and the grain looks cool when you drawknife the bark off. By using ash, you also may be making furniture from a wood that may soon be a rarity in America. The emerald ash borer is working its way across the Eastern U.S., killing every ash in its path. As I am writing this, there is no known cure to stop this invasive insect. It is very possible that ash will go the way of the American chestnut. For this reason, do not move ash logs, as you can be part of the problem. If you have ash on your property and you are making the furniture for your own use, there's no problem. If you are planning on selling the furniture, it may need to be inspected and certified, which costs money. Contact your state forestry division to find out what the laws are in your area.

Sugar maple

A favorite of rustic chair makers, this tree stays small in the heavy forest until something happens to the forest canopy, providing it with sunlight. There can be hundreds per acre just waiting for their chance to shine, so take all you want. It has been my experience that some peel easy and some peel hard, but once they dry they don't peel at all, so only cut what you can peel that day. (This tree is also the king of maple syrup. A good sugar maple over 10" (250 mm) in

Ash makes a beautiful bed, but it is extremely heavy.

46

diameter is prime for tapping, and you haven't lived until you've had fresh maple syrup.)

Red cedar

Bring up the topic of log furniture, and the most talked-about wood is red cedar. (Its shorter cousins, the Rocky Mountain and western juniper, grow in abundance in the western U.S.) This tree is a favorite for cedar chests, closet linings, and a hundred other geegaws in souvenir shops in the Smokies.

Eastern cedar grows taller and straighter than junipers found in the west, but for bed-size trees there isn't much difference. While both are native to their areas, they are often considered an invasive species because they are the first trees to retake a fallow field. They also readily spread into native grasslands that crowd out the native plants if a fire doesn't sweep through to kill them back.

The night stand is a mix of red cedar lumber and log quarters.

Red cedar and western juniper are a favorite of cabin owners.

Cedar is well known for its fragrance, which is said to repel insects that eat cloth. Some Native American ceremonies use the smoke from burning cedar boughs to purge evil spirits from an area.

Traditionally "hope chests," or trunks used by young women to store away important items for marriage, were made of cedar. Over the years some very plain cedar bedroom furniture (wardrobes, chests of drawers, vanity desks) have been produced commercially. An alert shopper at yard sales, flea markets, and auctions will find pieces of this furniture. Usually it's in poor repair or covered with gaudy paint. While originally plain, these pieces can be perfect for the addition of log details. If refinished and modified nicely with an artist's touch, they can add a great deal of western flair to a bedroom.

Red cedar has a beauty and character that can't be duplicated by artificial means.

Cedar is a softwood, like pines, spruce, and fir. The wood doesn't stand up well to abuse. Generally, furniture components that are load-bearing will need to be larger than if hickory was used. In most cases, this isn't an issue.

If you can find cedar logs large enough to be cut into lumber, grab them. Cedar plank table tops are gorgeous.

You can peel cedar easily in the early summer for a nice clean look. However, for that classic rustic cedar look, I put my logs on the ground for a few months and let the insects help me out. Since cedar is rot and insect resistant, the bugs work their way under the bark, making the log surface look distressed without causing structural harm to the log itself. To me, the distressed look is hands-down better than the clean, sterile look.

Contrary to popular opinion, cedar will rot. The sapwood will start rotting first, so keep an eye on wood lying on the ground. When the bark starts to slip, clean it up and store it in a dry location.

Another nice thing about cedar is that it shrinks less than any other wood.

White cedar

Grown as an ornamental in many areas of the U.S., white cedar grows naturally in many northern states. It is used extensively in the log home trade. Like red cedar it has natural insect resistance, but it doesn't have the red heartwood. To me, it looks boring. I've never cut enough to give the insect trick a try, but it might help.

Tulip poplar/yellowwood

The perfect log furniture wood. Yellowwood, as it's now being touted, is as close as it gets to perfect for us furniture makers. It's light, straight, fast growing, easy to peel, easy to work, and looks great. The bark comes off faster than a pop diva with a wardrobe malfunction. It has a nice yellow color that turns brown if allowed to sit outside with the bark off.

As one of the first trees to come back after logging, it grows fast with an almost perfect column straightness. Mr. Obvious says all trees grow smaller in girth as they gain height. Some trees do so faster than others—cedar is maddeningly so. At the base of a cedar log it can be 8" (200 mm) in diameter. Six feet (1.8 m) up it can be 4" (100 mm) in diameter. This pyramid shape is hard to work with. Yellowwood gains diameter more slowly than any tree I have worked with, making it as close to a milled log as nature allows. This column shape makes for easy matching of wood. Yellowwood is also light in comparison to other woods. Make a king headboard of ash and you better have help to move it. Make the same headboard from yellowwood and you'll notice a big difference.

The only drawback is the fact that yellowwood likes to put out random leaves along the trunk. When the log is peeled, each spot where a leaf grew has a thorn. These thorns are sharp and have to be removed. Go easy while taking them off or you will damage the surrounding wood, which you will have to sand, and which will take away from the natural surface of the log.

Black locust

Each spring, black locust trees have millions of hanging white flowers and were popular with farmers for rot-resistant fence posts. Relatively straight and easy to peel, this tree has a light sapwood and unique greenish-black

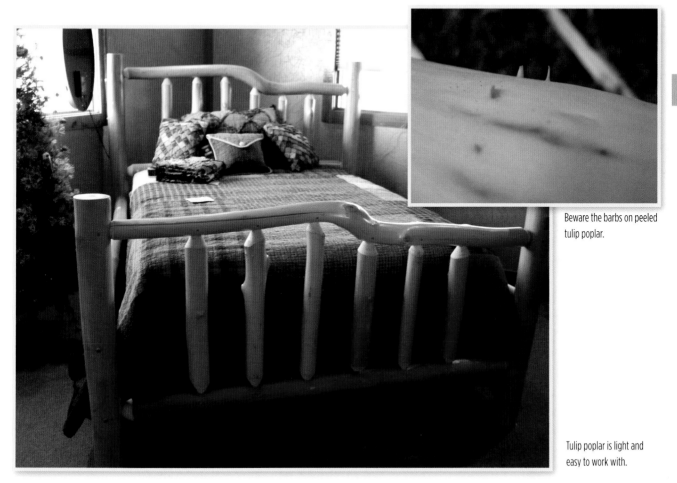

Beware the barbs on peeled tulip poplar.

Tulip poplar is light and easy to work with.

heartwood. It grows in clumps, so if you find one, you'll find more nearby. None of the locust logs I cut and peeled ever developed mold. They also experienced very little checking. The peeled wood has a very rough texture that can be appealing. But, black locust is very heavy.

Hickory

While it looks great with the bark on, hickory also peels extremely easy. After getting a slit in the bark started, the log can often be pried out in seconds, often with the bark staying in one piece. The inner log surface has a very interesting texture like no other wood I have seen.

Bigtooth aspen

Also known as poplar, this tree is found across the northern portion of the eastern U.S. Fast growing, this tree is one of the first to come back after a forest fire or logging. Like cedar, this wood is much more exciting after being distressed by insects and mold. Its snowy white wood turns gray and silver as mold and insects attack. Add wonderfully interesting defects and figure and you have a very popular wood for furniture. However, in the humid eastern U.S. it also rots very quickly. The best bet is to painstakingly peel it so it can dry quickly, or allow it to dry in a well-ventilated barn or shed to keep moisture off it.

Quaking and bigtooth aspen are well known in the western mountains and in the northern states. Both make interesting furniture.

Pine, the universal log furniture wood

Few of the trees listed in this book grow everywhere in North America. Excluding ornamental yard trees, climate and soil type dictate what tree can be found there. You won't find aspen trees in Florida. You won't find hickory in Arizona. You won't find sassafras in Wyoming.

Pine is the only family that is found coast to coast. Sure, they may vary from the vast ponderosa pine forests of Arizona to the lodgepole pines of Montana to the slash pine glades of Florida, but they all can make log furniture.

Even if you happen to be in an area where pines are hard to find, there is a singular event each year that provides millions of furniture-sized pine logs (as well as fir and spruce) to an enterprising furniture maker. Starting December 26th, millions of households are trying to figure what to do with their old Christmas tree. Lots of unsold Christmas trees can be had for the taking. Yes, they will have a gazillion branches to deal with and enough pine sap to ruin several sets of work clothes, but they are free.

Another way to get pine logs is to work with forest and wildlife managers. They have a running battle with the thick stands of pine saplings that grow tall and spindly and crowd out sunlight to the forest floor. Often they use controlled burns to kill off the small trees and undergrowth. This allows more sunlight to the ground so that native grasses and mast-producing plants can grow and support more wildlife. Your cutting of pine trees can actually help turkey, deer, elk, quail, and hundreds of other species of animals.

The point of this is, if you put in a little time and effort, you should be able to find pine, even if no other wood can be found.

Like other trees, pine can be peeled easily during the spring. An issue I have found is that the tree oozes sap, coating the freshly peeled surface with a sticky mess. Pine is one of the few trees that I prefer to allow to fully dry before working with.

Tiny pines grow into king-sized beds.

This white pine has limbs large enough to use for furniture.

Yard Furniture

Buyers sometimes ask if it's all right to place the furniture outside, exposed to the weather. The answer is yes and no. Yes, if you don't mind watching it rot away. No, if you want to keep it nice. Most commercially made yard furniture has been treated with chemicals to slow the destructive powers of insects and rot. The best natural choices for log furniture that will be outside are cedar and black locust.

I strongly recommend against using any wood that still has the bark on. Bark gives a great hiding place for wood-eating insects, and it helps trap moisture that in turn allows ants, termites, and rot to thrive.

Yes, you can cover the logs with polyurethane. And then you can watch the coating peel off like corn flakes in the sun.

CHAPTER 9
WORKING WITH LOGS

*O*nce your logs are on the ground, the work begins. Do as much of this work as you can in the woods before moving the logs. The bark and slash decays and feeds those new trees around it. I often pile my slash to make habitat for small game.

Bucking (debranching) the log is the first step. A chain saw can make quick work of this, but it can also create more problems if you're not careful. Damaged bark and saw nicks in the wood are common. While not as macho as a chain saw, a big pruning shear makes easy work of branches up to 1½" (40 mm) in diameter. A sharp pruning saw works well on those larger branches.

Peeling logs is also best done in the woods. Early summer is the best time to cut and peel logs. The bark is as loose as it gets. Some species are easier to peel than others, and even that varies from tree to tree. I have cut maple saplings within twenty feet (6 m) of each other; one peeled relatively easily, whereas one was so hard to peel it got chucked back into the brush. Yellowwood and hickory are extremely easy to peel, often only taking seconds to strip a log.

There are special tools for peeling logs, called bark spuds. They are used for peeling logs for log homes. Don't waste your money on them; they don't work well on small logs and they damage the wood. The best tool for peeling bark in the summer is a dull putty knife. I know a putty knife doesn't sound as cool as a rugged, manly bark spud. Trust me; the lowly putty knife works better than anything else I have found.

If you decide to peel fall- and winter-cut logs, you have your work cut out for you. Every well-meaning handyman will tell you bark comes off easily with a drawknife. Don't believe it. The reason God rested on the seventh day is that he used a drawknife on the sixth day. There is nothing easy about using a drawknife. Every branch, knot, or burl is a catching point. Let's not even talk about what happens when you dig too deep. Can it be done? Yes. Is it quick and easy? NO!

If you're a tool jock and plan on peeling lots of logs, I have a secret weapon. Makita makes a curved base planer specifically for working with logs. This planer makes peeling straight logs ridiculously easy. Hours of work can be done in minutes and looks the same as if you spent weeks with a drawknife.

As I said before, when peeling logs, it is best to work in the woods so that you can leave the bark where it falls. But, when that isn't possible, a nice shady part of the yard works well. There will be a mess no matter what you do. To anyone that has a fear of hornets and wasps, beware. The fresh wet logs and bark attract yellow jackets and other unwanted stinging guests.

Moving logs is the hardest part of the job. Driving right up to them with a pickup is wonderful but not always possible. An ATV or lawn tractor can drag logs, but keep in mind that any dirt and mud that is picked up has to be scrubbed off before using. Dragging can also make unsightly scrapes on the logs.

Lastly, there's the old-fashioned way to move logs. On the days I'm feeling froggy, I put them on my shoulder and walk them through the woods to my truck or shop, one at a time. On the days I'm feeling *really* froggy, I carry one on each shoulder. Remember to lift with your knees, find the balance point, and use a shoulder pad.

Storing logs really eats up space. With rare exceptions, the logs need to be protected from moisture, and they need to dry. Allowing the logs to touch the ground is a bad idea. Any dirt contact allows the wood to wick moisture, start decay, and provide a path for termites.

A horizontal rack works well for drying, but not so well when you need a log on the bottom.

Many folks like to build an elevated platform and lean their logs vertically against a wall. I take my logs into my conditioned shop and store them horizontally in racks or lean them against a wall. I try to keep them separated according to species so I can quickly see how much wood I have for a project.

Your work area needs to be large enough to swing logs around in, some of them eight feet (2.4 m) long or longer. A crowded workshop with low-hanging lights can make for some exciting moments.

Avoid anything that can distress your logs. At this point, any dent, slash, or cut is a blemish you have to deal with. Don't drop the logs to the hard cement floor. Don't kick them around with steel-toe boots. Don't knock them together or apart with a hammer. These are all things I did before I learned what damage they can do to the logs.

Case in point: While I was working with the logs for my first cedar bed, I chucked the logs onto the bumpy floor of my garage. While I drilled the mortise holes in the logs, I kicked them around with much bumping and grinding against the knots and branches of the other logs. To get the tenons to fit into the mortises, I smacked them with much bravado and a small sledgehammer, thinking

all the time that I would just sand out any imperfections I caused. Brother, I did not realize how much damage I was doing, nor how much work it was going to take to get it sanded out.

When I got around to sanding out all those dents and dings I foolishly put in, I used our old porch deck as a workbench. I sanded and sanded those logs, turning them over and over, trying to get rid of every nick I found. After a time period longer than I care to admit to, I realized I was resanding areas that I had already completed before. In puzzlement, I picked the logs up to see what was causing the new nicks and scratches. There, on the old deck boards, were multiple nail heads protruding just enough to do more damage as I rolled the logs around. A piece of old shag carpeting cured that issue.

Now I treat each log as if it were a rotten egg ready to break.

Enter the sawbuck, a cradle device to hold logs while being cut or cleaned. A sawbuck is something you can easily build to suit your needs. Plans for building a sawbuck are plentiful on the Internet. I made mine tall enough to work logs without bending over, and my back thanks me every time I use it.

Keeping your wood organized by species helps to keep track of what wood is available. Notice the massive section of tulip poplar bark in the center.

CHAPTER 10
INSECTS—FRIEND OR FOE?

Most insects are a foe. Termites and carpenter ants can be quick to move into any logs you have touching the ground. Generally, they need the wood to have a high moisture content to get started and survive. Here in the Midwest, they are dormant during the winter, which is another good reason to harvest logs then. Good log hygiene keeps these pests from becoming a problem.

Ambrosia beetles are a small, common wood borer. They love to burrow into freshly cut logs. A telltale sign is small piles of dust that pile up below their holes or their stacks of waste that extrude from their burrow holes. Don't get too excited about ambrosia beetles. They only thrive in moist wood, so as the log dries, they die or move on. The good thing is that the boreholes give logs a distressed look that many folks love.

Ambrosia beetles can quickly bore into fresh wood, but die as the wood dries.

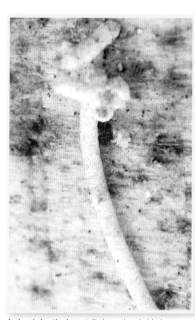

Ambrosia beetles leave telltale castings behind.

Powderpost beetles can be your worst nightmare. Powderpost damage is common on the beams of old houses and barns and can be easily recognized by the pin-sized holes that can be seen as they enter and leave the wood. These small wood borers are a bane to all woodworkers. They have no problem living in dry wood, and their life cycle can take years to complete. They are divided into two species, one that likes softwood and one that likes hardwood. Generally, once softwood powderpost beetles hatch, they burrow out looking for more softwood. The same is true for hardwood-loving powderpost beetles; they look for more hardwood. The crazy thing is that some antique lovers want powderpost damage on their rare treasures! Some dealers even take a shotgun to furniture to give it that same insect-distressed look.

Metallic/flathead borers can make interesting tunnels just under the bark of aspen and poplar trees. Much of the rustic aspen furniture made has designs made by these insects. The problem here in the humid Midwest is rot setting in before the beetles are done with your logs.

Cedar bark beetles are my friends. I purposely leave my bark-on cedar logs on the ground for six months or more so they can do their thing. The beetles make interesting designs just under the bark that really give it that sought-after distressed look, and the beetles help loosen the bark for when I'm ready to strip it off.

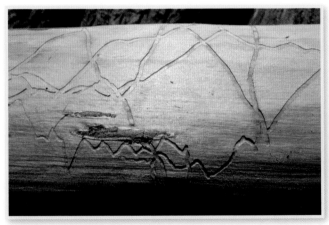

Flathead borers leave tracks just under the bark on aspen trees. The distressed look is nice and doesn't affect the integrity of the log enough to matter.

Cedar bark beetles do not harm the wood, and their bore marks look cool. They also help loosen the bark.

Making Your Logs Insect Free

There are two ways to kill these insects. The first is to kiln-dry all your wood and bring the interior wood temperature up to 130 degrees Fahrenheit (55°C). The high heat will cook the eggs, larva, and beetles. Problem solved.

Another way is to chemically kill them with borates. These clear wood treatments have been used for years in the log home industry. The borate compound penetrates deep into the untreated wood and kills any insects, mold, or mildew. A protective coating like polyurethane can be placed over the borate after it is dry.

Borates are chemicals that treat wood to kill insects and prevent another infestation. They are widely used in the log home industry.

Mildew, Rot, and Mold

Wood is much like a sponge. The millions of cells hold water, and given the right circumstances mold, rot, and mildew will start. Mostly, mold and mildew are not a big problem to peeled logs as long as they are allowed to dry. In most cases, it is best to dry the wood as fast as possible. Twenty-percent moisture content is the magic number. Above that and rot can grow. Below that, you're golden. (That means good.) If you know what length logs your project requires, it is best to cut your logs close to that length. The shorter the log, the faster it can dry.

If the log has been freshly debarked and is still wet, wash any sap and sugars off the log and place them in the sun to dry the surface quickly. If it is summertime, you can carefully arrange them over your air conditioner condensing unit outside. Take care not to block the airflow. The hot air coming off the condensing unit can quickly dry out your logs.

Another trick is to stack your logs in a weather-protected area and place an oscillating fan to blow on them.

If you do find mold growing on the surface of a peeled log, it's no big deal. Generally, the mold can be brushed or wiped away. If left too long the mold can stain the surface, but again, this adds to the rustic distressed look that so many folks love.

Rot is bad. The structural strength of the wood is gone when rot starts. You might as well throw the log away and learn a lesson on drying wood.

Spalting is good. Many woodworkers pay big bucks for spalting. What is spalting? It is nature's reward for the alert woodsmith. Spalting is the first stage of rot. Mildew sets in and creates a fine black spiderweb of lines in the wood. Drying the wood at that point keeps the wood strong and gives you some incredibly beautiful designs.

As I said before, I like to stack my cedar logs on the ground and let nature do its thing. Cedar is more forgiving than other woods due to its resistance to rot and insects, so the window of opportunity to get good wood is much longer. The usual result is wonderful staining and spalting. Try the same thing with aspen and you get a pile of mulch.

Spalting is one of nature's gifts.

Spalted wood can be very expensive on the open market.

CHAPTER 11
DRYING WOOD

No wood should be used before it's completely dry for multiple reasons. But, the drying process can take time if you don't have a kiln.

If you talk to many woodworkers on the topic of drying wood, it won't be long before the old rule of thumb comes up; figure a year for every inch (25 mm) of thickness, if the wood is kept out of the weather.

I have found that rule to be safe, but not totally accurate. Some woods dry faster than others. Some woods have a naturally lower moisture content than others to start with. Some woods have a moisture content of 70 to 90 percent when cut during the wet, growing season! Which is why we want to *cut the wood in the right season.*

Logs with bark on them dry slower than logs without bark. I mean, that is the point of bark: to protect the tree from bumps, abrasions, weather, varmints, drought, etc. Imagine the bark as a layer of plastic coating that holds moisture in, because, in reality, it is. With drying some woods, rot may set in before it gets to the "safe zone" of moisture content.

Woods that are denser dry slower than woods that are less dense. For example, inch for inch, ash will dry slower than poplar.

Generally speaking, wood wicks moisture out of the ends of the log. This is because of the cellular structure of wood. It's easiest to think of a log as a bundle of soda straws. Moisture is sucked out at the ends of the straw, not the sides.

Moisture tries to seek a balance. If a log or board is stood upright in a bucket of water, the cell structure will wick the water up into the board, just like a towel wicks water. The reverse is also true. If kept in the dry air, the moisture wicks away until the moisture content of the board matches the moisture content of the air. Once they match, the board is done drying and stable.

The shorter the log, the less time it takes to dry.

Making a Kiln

Kiln-drying wood speeds up the process of drying. There are different types of kilns, from simple to complex. To understand the process of drying wood, you need to understand the principles of relative humidity. The warmer air is, the more moisture it will hold. The greater the difference in moisture content, the more rapid the exchange of moisture will be. So, while wood will dry in the workshop's ambient air, it will dry faster if the air is heated. Moisture seeks equilibrium, so the larger the difference is in humidity, the faster the transfer will be.

The problem is that once the air absorbs all the moisture it can, it needs to be removed, and fresh air replaces it. Think of it this way: A towel is used to pick up a large water spill. The dry towel absorbs the water until the towel is saturated and can't hold more water. At that

59

point, a new towel needs to replace it. Air is the same way. The best way to achieve this air transfer is to have a small fan slowly extract air from the kiln and allow fresh air to replace it.

There are ways to heat the kiln, but the most economical way is to have the sun do it. Many hobby woodworkers build a solar kiln, much like a greenhouse. The sunlight heats the air in the kiln. Since the air can now hold more moisture, it draws moisture from the wood. The fan removes the hot moist air. Fresh cool air enters and the process continues.

A desired feature on kilns is to heat the wood to 135 degrees Fahrenheit (57°C) or higher. Along with drying the wood, the high temperatures also sterilize it and kill any bugs and larvae in it. This is a great way to kill any powderpost beetles that may have bored into the log or wood.

Another way to dry the wood is to dehumidify it. A dehumidifier uses the process of refrigeration to pull moisture from the air. The air is drawn into the dehumidifier. As the air travels across the cold evaporator coil, moisture is drawn from the air and condenses on the cold coil. The water then drips off and is captured in a tank or goes down a drain. As the dry air continues on, it blows across the hot condenser coil, which heats the already dry air, which decreases the relative humidity before blowing it out into the kiln. The hot dry air absorbs moisture and reruns to the dehumidifier to start the process all over.

A dehumidifier kiln can also be made. I had an old dehumidifier that I placed inside a urethane foam coffin box I had built over a floor drain. The box was four feet (1.2 m) wide by four feet (1.2 m) tall by eight feet (2.4 m) long with a lumber frame to hold up the two-inch (50 mm) thick urethane panels. I placed the logs and dehumidifier into the box and allowed the dehumidifier to operate. Every week I would open the lid and check the logs with a moisture meter. Within a month, the logs were dry and ready to use. While the kiln dried the logs well, it never reached a temperature high enough to kill powderpost beetles.

Any kiln you make needs to be large enough to handle the wood you are going to be using, small enough to be efficient, and air-tight enough that you have control of the drying process.

You need to decide what process will work for you, air-drying or kiln-drying. Each has its rewards and drawbacks. Air-drying is a long process and requires patience. Kiln-drying requires an investment in space and supplies. Plus, many steam benders believe that kiln-dried wood doesn't bend as well as air-dried. After experimentation, I have decided to air-dry my wood.

I recommend reading *Principles and Practices of Drying Lumber* by Eugene M. Wengert for more information on drying wood.

CHAPTER 12
FINDING NATURE'S GIFTS

I love walking in the woods looking for just the right trees for a project. The problem is, I often get sidetracked by all the beautiful and interesting things that most folks pass by without noticing. Some might be as subtle as a turkey track in a mud puddle or the flattened leaves where a deer had lain. Other times it might be an antler shed dropped by a nice buck late last winter or a patch of wild blackberries ripening on the cane. All of these are a gift from Mother Nature to the alert searcher.

Some of nature's gifts are great for decorating or for use in furniture. The only problem is, some of these "gifts" are very rare. It has taken me years of saving certain unusual items to get enough to make a cohesive piece. I am providing a short list to get the ol' brain gears working. With time and experience, there's no end to what special things nature provides if you keep your eyes open.

Antler rubs make already-beautiful pieces even more special.

Antler rubs

In the fall of the year, during the mating season, male deer and elk go into a period called the "rut." At the beginning of the rut, the male deer and elk rub the dead skin and fuzz off their new antlers by taking their aggressions out on trees and brush. In doing so, the antlers rub away the bark. In almost all cases the tree is damaged. As the tree struggles to survive, it works to heal the area by slowly covering it with bark. In some cases, the blaze (damage) made by past deer attracts new generations of deer to rub their antlers in the same location. The damage, known as rubs to hunters and naturalists, are a visual reminder of the majesty of male deer or elk. In many cases, male deer will make a rub line or series of rubs as they mark their territory. Collecting these rubs can make furniture exciting to any hunter.

Every spindle in this headboard is an antler rub.

Vine damage

Japanese honeysuckle is an invasive vine that was brought over as an ornamental flower. It is one of the plants that are the bane of any tree farmer because as a vine it rapidly climbs to the top of the forest canopy and shades out the valuable trees underneath. In the process, the vines often wind around their host. As the tree tries to grow, the tree either envelops the vine or dies. These trees will have a spiral pattern in the bark and may even cause a twist to the tree. Wood carvers prize the younger saplings for use as fancy walking sticks. Larger trees make interesting legs or spindles in a bed headboard.

As vines like Japanese honeysuckle climb a sapling, it often causes the tree to form a twist pattern that is popular among cane carvers. They can also make interesting spindles.

Healed wounds

Like all the other interesting finds listed before, wounds can be interesting in furniture in two ways. If the tree is small enough, the wound can be part of the piece. If it is on a larger log, the wound areas can be cut as part of an interesting and beautiful slab for tabletops.

A heavy storm can damage multiple trees in the same stand. The upper rails on this bed were damaged in a heavy storm, then started growing again.

Old crotches

In most cases, trees grow with a single trunk. On rare occasions, something causes the tree to branch off into separate distinct main beams. As the tree grows, the beams continue to grow in diameter until they reach each other, then all growth in that direction stops, making a crotch. As the tree continues to grow, the sapwood in the crotch turns to heartwood. The anomaly of heartwood growing right up to the bark can be beautiful. The funny thing is that commercial lumber mills don't want the crotch area, so the loggers leave them where they fall and just take the clear wood before and after it. Your only problem is finding a way to get the crotch to someone with a Wood-Mizer setup.

This crotched black cherry is worthless to veneer buyers but is a gold mine to log furniture artists.

Flame box elder

This "gift" is like a Christmas snow in the desert. It is special and lovely while it lasts. Older box elder trees are often in distress from insects. The distress causes flames of red streaks in the wood which can be unbelievably beautiful if cut into planks or slabs. But, the beauty is fleeting. After the wood is exposed to light, the brilliant red flames fade, leaving faint yellow streaks.

Downed logs

While massive trees look as unmoving as the Rock of Gibraltar, it doesn't take much of a wind storm to blow trees over. While it's frustrating to lose a mature tree to a storm, it can be a gift in disguise; after all, the tree is already on the ground. If the tree is large enough, nice slabs can be cut for tabletops.

If you do find a freshly downed tree, you have two options. The first and perhaps easiest option is to cut it into workable sections and get it to a local sawyer with a Wood-Mizer band-saw setup.

The second option requires a great deal of work, but it might be the only viable option if you can't move or transport the log. Procure or borrow a chainsaw lumber mill. They take a great deal of setup to start cutting and

Insect damage can cause box elder trees to produce a red coloring. The wood is known as flame box elder. Enjoy it while it lasts. The red quickly fades in sunlight.

each cut can take an eternity, but they do work and the lumber and slabs that are produced are much easier to move and transport.

Do not dillydally in getting the log cut and drying. In many parts of the country, the log can quickly start to deteriorate and become unsalvageable within months.

CHAPTER 13
STEAM BENDING

*Y*ou can see steam-bent wood around you every day. In many cases, you may not have recognized it. Steam bending is an ancient craft and can be an art form in itself. What is steam bending, you ask? It is the practice of using heat to bend wood.

Think of the cells in wood as a bundle of drinking straws that are glued together. The glue that binds wood together is known as lignin. Under normal circumstances, lignin is very stiff, but if it is heated to 212 degrees Fahrenheit (100°C) or higher, the lignin becomes soft and pliable. By heating wood and then placing it in a form, it can be bent into desired shapes. The great thing is that the wood loses very little of its natural strength in the process.

A simple form holds the wood as it cools.

There are some simple truths about steam bending. You will need a heat source to safely make steam. You will need a container in which to boil water into steam. You will need to pipe the steam into a container large enough to hold the wood you want to bend.

There are many ways to make a steam bender. There are even premade units that can be bought ready to go. I am going to focus on my setup because it is made with easy-to-buy parts. My heat source is a flea market find and is a 120-volt (mains voltage) electric hotplate, large enough to hold a kettle. My boiler is an old pressure cooker that I also found at a flea market. My container is a section of four-inch (100 mm) PVC pipe.

In my setup, I removed the pressure gauge from the pressure cooker lid and used the hole to install ⅜" (10 mm) copper tubing. The copper tubing runs a short distance to a hole drilled in the PVC pipe. The open ends of the PVC are closed off with wood blocks. **The blocks are NOT held in place.** They merely hold the heat in. The PVC pipe is supported by a board . . . because heat will allow PVC to bend.

A word of caution: Boiling water into steam in an enclosed container can produce explosive results. Do nothing that will confine the steam without an outlet to release pressure. The pressure cooker has a factory pressure relief valve. Test it by manually popping it off before using the unit. The wood blocks at the ends of the PVC tube are not held in place and are easily moved so no pressure can build up.

A steam bender is a simple device used to soak wood in hot steam so it can be bent. The steam is generated in the pressure cooker, travels through the copper tube, and fills the PVC pipe, heating the sapling. Once it's hot all the way through, it will easily bend.

Bark may also need to be steamed to bend or flatten properly.

Think before you build your steam bender. Make sure your piping is sized to allow steam to escape the boiler as fast as it is being made. Make sure nothing will allow pressure to build up. Even a small increase in pressure can cause a problem. If the pressure relief is constantly venting, that's a warning sign that the boiler is producing too much steam. Lower the heat to the unit.

Remember that hot water and steam can scald very easily. Make sure the entire setup is stable and won't tip over when handling the hot wood or cause an uncontrolled release of steam.

To bend wood, the piece needs to be heated all the way through. Think of it as a steak. If all you do is sear the outside, the inside won't be hot enough to bend properly. The wood needs to be "well-done" and heated all the way through. The smaller the wood thickness, the faster it will be ready to bend. Experience will be your guide, but figure 30–60 minutes to heat the wood.

If you plan on keeping the bark on, limit the bend to a gradual arc, otherwise the bark may split. Beware pressure points from clamps and forms as they may also cause the bark to split.

There are no hard and fast rules on steam bending. Some pieces will bend easier than others, even of the same species. Knots and defects will also affect how the wood will bend.

Once the wood is up to temperature, remove it and get it into the form as fast as possible. Wear thick welding gloves to protect your hands from the superheated wood.

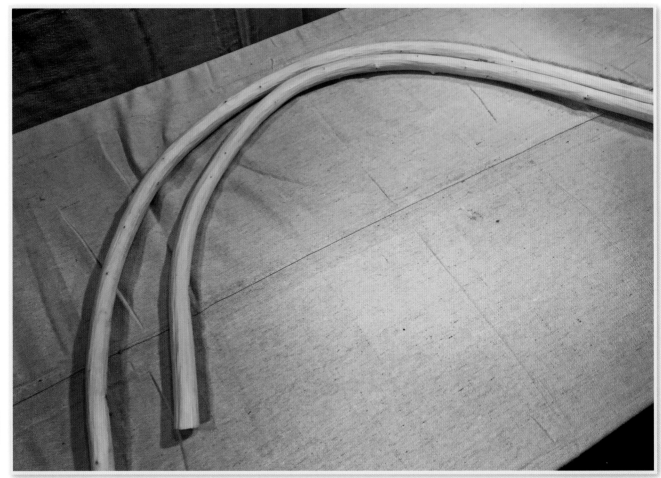

Removing the wood from the form too soon can allow it to spring back. The top piece was removed from the form after 15 minutes. The bottom piece stayed in the form until the next morning.

Get it in the jig and clamped as fast as humanly possible because the wet wood will evaporate and cool rapidly. As it cools, its ability to bend decreases.

Leave the wood in the jig until it is cool. I recommend leaving it until the next day if possible. A general guideline for cooling is 45–60 minutes. If you remove it too soon, more than normal spring back can occur. Spring back is where a piece of wood tries to go back to the original shape.

Plan on some spring back on all bends. Knowing that some spring back will occur, the bend will need to be greater than the desired results. There are no hard and fast rules, as it varies from species to species and even piece to piece. If it is critical that the two pieces have to match, make more than you need in hopes that you can get some to match.

There are limits to how tight a radius of the bend can be. Since we are dealing with whole limbs, it will be hard to bend without breaking. If a tight bend is required but the wood keeps breaking, redesign the project to use multiple smaller limbs in the place of one larger limb.

If you really enjoy bending wood, make a dedicated bending table with holes for dog clamps and radius jigs. If you have the time, skills, and equipment, steam bending can become an art form itself.

CHAPTER 14
FASTENING/ JOINING WOOD

Unless you just turn a section of log on end to use as a table or stool, you will need to learn how to fasten logs and planks together in a manner that looks pleasing to the beholder, yet holds the piece together against the rigors of use. At its most basic terms, these two rules have to be followed every time. If they are not followed, the piece will appear unsightly or will fall apart.

The first step is to make surfaces that match well. If a 1" (25 mm) tenon is placed into a 2" (250 mm) mortise, no amount of nails, screws, or glue is going to make the joint pleasing to look at, and I doubt it will be strong. Poorly made tenons will detract from a piece, while well-made tenons will often enhance it.

> ✓ TIP
>
> Make the tenon cuts match in length. If they differ too much it will detract from the piece.

A radius tenon looks good on exposed trim work.

Tenons

A tenon is defined as a projecting piece of wood used to make a wood joint. These days, most log furniture joints are made with a round tenon, which is inserted into a round hole, known as a mortise.

At its most basic, a woodworker could measure the diameter of a stick and drill a matching hole, no fancy tools required. Many of our ancestors whittled a tenon to match a mortise. These days we have a vast array of tenon cutters to choose from. The two most common styles are cutting bits used with an electric drill.

One style produces a straight-angled pencil sharpener–like tenon; the other style produces a rounded radius tenon. There are pros and cons to each.

The two common tenon cutters are "pencil sharpener" (top) style and radius (bottom) style. Both have a use.

Size the tenon to match the job. I use 1½" (40 mm) or 2" (50 mm) tenons on headboard rails and 1" (25 mm) or 1½" (40 mm) tenons on headboard spindles. Tables or benches get 1" (25 mm) or 1½" (40 mm) tenons for the legs and ⅝" (16 mm) tenons for braces and trim pieces.

Tenons don't have to be round. Many pieces of furniture also use square tenons. The drawback is that you will need to manually cut the mortise with a chisel. From personal experience, there's nothing fast about cutting a mortise by hand in hardwood.

Using a countersink bit allows pencil sharpener tenons (top) to seat better and provide more gluing surface if desired. Radius cutters (bottom) produce a cleaner, more traditional look. I prefer to use a pencil sharpener type tenon for larger, load-bearing joints and a radius type tenon on decorative joints.

> ## ✓ TIP
> If you want to shift a tenon off center, cut away part of the log tip to shift the cutter over. The tenon cutter will center itself over the remaining log section.

PENCIL SHARPENER–STYLE TENON CUTTER

- **Pros:** When used with a matching countersink bit, a very strong joint can be produced. The rough shank provides a great glue-holding surface. Some manufacturers produce cutters with movable knives and shank inserts so that one cutter can produce multiple-size tenons. The blades are easy to sharpen.

- **Con:** The rough shank looks unprofessional when left exposed.

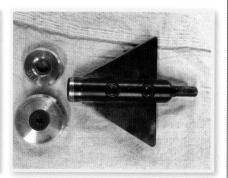

These pencil sharpener–style tenon cutters center up on the log better. The tenon length can be set by adjusting the shaft.

A countersink bit provides a better tenon fit and a professional look.

RADIUS TENON CUTTER

- **Pros:** The tenon radius and shank is smooth and visually appealing. The radius tenon has a very traditional look many buyers like.

- **Cons:** Each cutter only does one size, making a set of cutters very expensive. The cutter is hard to get started on larger pieces. I find I need to start the cut with a pencil sharpener–style cutter, then finish it with a radius cutter. The blade takes more skill to sharpen.

A good selection of tenon cutters is key to producing a professional product.

✓ TRICK

If a radius-style cutter is difficult to start on a log, use a pencil sharpener–style cutter until the tenon is started, then switch back to the radius cutter.

A word on tenon cutters: Cutters try to center themselves on the end of the log as they turn. If a log has a deformity that swells the end of the log in an eccentric, offset fashion, it will shift the tenon and cause it to also be offset from center. If this is the case, before starting the tenon, use a bandsaw to remove the swelling and make the log end concentric. Then the tenon will be center of the log.

Dowel Pins

I used to use dowels exclusively. Every joint was made using oak dowels driven into pre-drilled holes filled with glue. It was very time-consuming. I thought it elevated my work to not use metal fasteners. The problem was, I had so many man-hours in each piece, nobody wanted to pay for the labor. Nobody made the connection between wooden dowels and quality. It didn't take long to find faster, yet equally strong ways to fasten joints.

Doweling a piece together is very time consuming, but it looks nice.

✓ TRICK

While radius tenon cutters produce great-looking results, they can be hard to start on larger logs. If you have ever tried starting a tenon like this, you know the cutter head can walk about and has a hard time starting the cut. It can even be dangerous.

This can be alleviated by tapering the end of the log to a point with a saw. By doing so, the tenon cutter stays centered on the point long enough that a tenon is formed. Once the tenon starts, the cutter head is held captive by the tenon itself.

✓ TRICK

No tenon or matching hole is ever perfectly aligned. If they bind or are pointed at an off angle as you are trying to assemble a piece, try turning the tenoned piece until you feel the joint loosen. There is almost always a sweet spot at which the tenon alignment is closer to perfect than at other spots. If the joint is really tight, you may need to take it back apart and reduce the diameter of the tenon. If you are having trouble turning a large tenon, a strap wrench can help without damaging the wood.

Cut larger logs to a sharp point with a saw to make starting tenons easier.

The radius tenon cutter naturally centers on the sharpened point.

Once started, the tenon cutter is held captive by the tenon itself.

HIDING MISTAKES

There are few things more frustrating than drilling a mortise by mistake. In most cases I throw the log in the scrap bin, get another piece, and start over. But, sometimes I have too much time invested in a piece to throw in the towel. In those cases, I try to repair my mistake by plugging the mortise with a matching piece of wood and blend it in as best I can.

A plug cutter is the easiest way to cut a plug. Plug cutters come in sets and can include sizes from ¼" (6 mm) up to 1" (25 mm) or more. They can be ordered from many woodworking and DIY supply companies.

If you don't want to spend money on a plug cutter or the size you need isn't available, a hole saw can be used for the same thing.

Keep in mind that a hole saw dimension is referring to the outside diameter of the saw, not the inside diameter. So if you want a 1" (25 mm) hole plug, you most likely will need a 1¹⁄₁₆" size (27 mm) hole saw.

The same goes for larger sizes. Generally speaking, you will need a hole saw ¹⁄₁₆" (1.5 mm) to ⅛" (3 mm) larger than the drill used to cut the mortise. For example, a 1½" (38 mm) mortise will need a 1⁹⁄₁₆" (39 mm) to 1⅝" (41 mm) hole saw for the proper size plug. You may need to do some sanding to get the plug to fit snugly, and as the hole saw gets worn, the plug size it cuts will change slightly.

- **To make a plug, remove the pilot drill bit from the hole saw adapter, otherwise you will have another hole to plug!**
- **Chuck the hole saw up in a drill press. I do not recommend trying this free-hand. The drill press keeps the hole saw from walking as the cut starts.**
- Select a piece of scrap log that matches the area to be repaired.
- Clamp the scrap piece of log down the drill press bed.
- Slowly cut into the log. A dull hole saw or cutting too fast can burn the wood.
- Once the hole saw is deep enough to form a sturdy plug, stop cutting and remove the saw.
- Use a sturdy screwdriver to pop the plug loose from the scrap piece of log.
- File and sand the plug just enough so that it snugly fits the mortise to be plugged.
- Once it's the size desired, glue the plug in place in a manner that closely matches the grain or contour of the log surface.

Use a hole saw without a pilot bit to cut a plug.

Pop the plug loose.

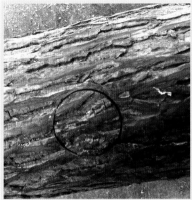

Carefully fit the plug into the hole and align the bark or grain pattern to look natural.

Normally a hole saw uses a pilot bit, as seen on the right. Remove it to cut plugs.

Cutting Tenons with Hole Saws

As long as we're on the topic of hole saws, they can serve another function: cutting tenons. Let's face reality, tenon cutters are expensive to the beginner woodworker. If you're like I am, you have more spare time than spare cash, so using hole saws might just be the route to get started making log furniture. Don't get too excited about the prospect of saving money because there is nothing fast or easy about using a hole saw as a tenon cutter.

As mentioned previously, you will need a hole saw a little larger than the mortise drill bit. A one-inch (25 mm) mortise will need a tenon cut with a one and one-sixteenth inch (27 mm) or one and one-eighth inch (29 mm) hole saw. This is because the hole saw is sized by its outside diameter, not the inside diameter. The thickness of the saw kerf generally removes a sixteenth (1.5 mm) to one-eighth inch (3 mm) of material. This will hold true on all sizes of hole saws.

Cut into the end of the log with a hole saw.

1. To cut a tenon with a hole saw, chuck up the hole saw adapter in a hand-held drill. Make sure the pilot drill bit is in place.

2. Place the log to be worked in a vise.

3. Drill/cut into the end of the log until you reach the end of the hole saw and the saw can no longer advance.

4. Remove the hole saw from the cut.

5. Using a saw, carefully cut around the log down to the end of the cut produced by the hole saw.

6. Remove the waste shell and discard.

7. The tenon is complete unless you want to taper the log down to the tenon. If you do, use a saw to remove sections of the log and finish by sanding.

The hole saw leaves a pilot hole, but no one will ever see it.

One of the drawbacks to using a hole saw to cut tenons is that the length of the tenon is limited by the depth of the hole saw.

Carefully cut around the log down to the hole saw cut.

Taper the log to the tenon with saw cuts and sanding.

Nails (and Why to Avoid Using Them)

Used in appropriate places, nails can be extremely useful and time saving. I use finishing nails as pins for braces. But, I pre-drill the hole and use a nail set to drive the head deep enough to hide the nail from casual observation. However, I avoid large nails like the plague. I have seen log furniture put together with common 16-penny (100 mm) nails. The furniture looks very unprofessional. Large nails act as a wedge, and as the wood dries, the log splits at the nail, rendering the joint worthless.

Nail Guns

I use pneumatic finish nail guns to speed up some processes. When working with bark and twigs, small brads dispensed with a pull of a trigger are invaluable. I use several sizes of nail guns so that the brad matches the job required.

In this make-it-faster world, pneumatic nail guns cut labor. Having a selection of sizes helps match the fastener to the job.

A tenon can be pinned together with large finishing nails inserted in pre-drilled undersized holes.

Lag Bolts

Large joints require large fasteners. The large components of bed headboards and tables are fastened using strong but stylish lag bolts, made by Hillman. The steel lag bolts are ceramic coated and have a star drive. They're strong, come in various lengths, and look great on rustic furniture.

Decorative lag bolts must be used on load-bearing joints like bed rails.

In some cases, large furniture is designed so that it can be disassembled for transport. One example would be bed frames. In most cases, the bed can be broken down into the headboard, the footboard, and the rails. In cases where log rails are used, they are tenoned and bolted to the head and foot boards with lag bolts. Let's face it, common lag bolts are unsightly, but the lag bolt heads can be covered with faux tenons that result in a design that makes it appear that the tenon passes all the way through the log. The technique is easy.

- Drill a mortise for the bed rail log.
- Starting at the bottom of the mortise, drill the rest of the way through the log with a small but long pilot drill bit.
- Changing back to a drill bit to match the original mortise, make a shallow mortise on the opposite side of the log by following the pilot hole.
- Leave enough wood between the mortises so that the lag bolt won't tear through as it is being tightened up.
- Using a tenon cutter on a piece of scrap wood, cut a tenon, then cut it off with a saw.
- Carefully sand the edges and fit it into the mortise that has the lag bolt head. Make sure the faux tenon is tight enough that it won't fall out but loose enough that it can be removed if the piece needs to be disassembled.
- When completed, it appears that the tenon passes all the way through the log.

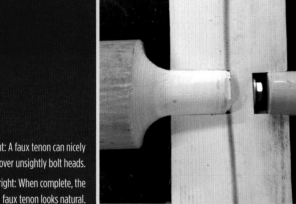

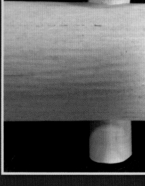

Right: A faux tenon can nicely cover unsightly bolt heads.
Far right: When complete, the faux tenon looks natural.

Screws

I use screws extensively. Most major joints are screwed together in some manner. My preferred screw is a strong deck screw that is driven by a star or square tip. Beware a smaller-diameter screw in hardwoods. It's easy to snap a weak screw off in wood like hickory, oak, and maple. Once the screw is broken off, it's often impossible to remove without damaging the piece.

Strong screws are invaluable during assembly work. I use a pilot hole to prevent splitting of the wood.

Biscuit Jointers

On some occasions, a piece calls for a solid top made from planks joined edge to edge, or a slab needs to be split, planed, and rejoined. In these instances, joints need something to aid in strength and alignment. It's hard to beat a biscuit joint. A biscuit joint is made by gluing a football-shaped piece of wood into matching slots on the edges of the boards to be joined. In a perfect world, the biscuit absorbs the moisture from the glue, expands into the slot, and dries. Biscuits come in different sizes to match the job at hand. I keep three sizes on hand: 00, 10, and 20.

A biscuit joint aids in making strong glue joints, such as on tabletops or chair seats.

Strap Wrench

Sometimes a tenon will go into a mortise easier by turning it. A strap wrench makes the task of turning the log easier.

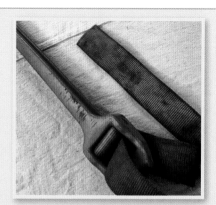

Turning a log will help find the sweet spot where pieces align better. A strap wrench works well without marring the wood.

CHAPTER 15
FINISHING YOUR ARTWORK

*A*fter all the blood, sweat, and tears you've put into a project, the last thing you'd want to happen is a bad finish. Ideally, a separate finishing booth is a great thing to have. Something with great lighting and an air filtration system and exhaust. Unfortunately, most of us do not have that luxury or garage space. On small projects, I do my finishing indoors. On large projects, I take it someplace with a great deal of ventilation and where overspray isn't going to land on something valuable, like a car.

A good finish enhances the qualities of the wood.

I recommend procuring a pop-up outdoor screen room. Why? Glad you asked. The day can look totally clear and still, with no clouds in sight, but the second you start shooting a finish on a project, a slight wind is going to kick up and every seed, needle, catkin, leaf, and twig within 100 yards (100 m) is going to land on your project. I swear that wood finish must smell like insect food, because any insect that can fly or hop will find your wet finish to get stuck on.

Make sure your work is out of direct sunlight. I learned this the hard way. I was trying to complete a coffee table in record time and I decided that shooting the top with polyurethane in direct sunlight would shorten the drying time. Bad idea. The sun heated the wood and started creating small bubbles anywhere there was a pore in the grain. Within 30 minutes, my table looked like it had a bad case of poison ivy blisters. My short-cut ended up costing me days. I had to strip off the polyurethane and start over again.

There are several ways to apply finish: brush, spray can, or High Volume, Low Pressure (HVLP) sprayer. Each has its benefits and drawbacks.

Finishing with a brush requires care that you don't mix paint bubbles into the surface. It also requires a foam brush and special bristle brush made for finishing. The bristle brush can be expensive. Foam brushes are cheap, but if a person isn't careful the foam can start to break

off and leave tiny bits on the surface. I usually reserve brushing for small surfaces or when the weather is too cold for me to allow good ventilation that spraying requires.

An HVLP rig is how many larger operations finish their projects, and for good reason. Two big reasons are the cost savings and the capacity. Finish isn't cheap, but you can lower the cost per ounce (ml) by buying it in gallon cans (or largest size available). By buying the finish in gallon cans the cost per ounce is cut in half or even less. And an HVLP sprayer is going to have capacity enough to hold 16–32 ounces (0.5–1 l) of finish. That should be enough for one coat on a king-size bed.

The downside of HVLP sprayers is the maintenance and cleanup. While it isn't a huge ordeal, it is enough of an issue in my shop that smaller projects are set aside until I have several to finish, or I resort to aerosol cans.

One last downside of using bigger cans of finish is that they tend to skin over and dry out, no matter how tight the lid goes back on.

Aerosol spray cans of finish are the most common way hobby woodworkers finish their work, and I am one of them. It is a matter of convenience. Since I'm almost always starting from a fresh can, I always have a new tip to use. The finish never dries out while sitting on the shelf. Plus, I don't have to do any cleanup. The only issue is the cost. An end table can take $15–$20 (£10–£15) of finish using aerosol cans.

79

A HVLP rig is useful for big projects, otherwise use aerosol cans.

To prevent clogs when using a HVLP machine, it's best to strain any finish. Spray tank liners help cleanup go faster.

POLYURETHANE VS. LACQUER

When you walk down the wood finish aisle at your favorite building supply store, you'll find a vast array of products, most of which are polyurethane-based. The rest are lacquer-based. Your next question is: What is the difference? Good question.

Lacquer is a resin-based finish. It takes a solvent to make it into a liquid. As the solvent dries, the resin hardens into a protective coating. In most applications, the solvent dries very fast. Professional furniture makers can coat a piece six to eight times in a day.

An advantage of lacquer is that the new coat liquefies the surface of the old coat, so they readily bond without sanding. Also, reworking the dried lacquer with the correct solvents can change it back into a liquid, just in case you need to repair a mistake. The fast dry time is also a plus when considering overspray. In most cases, any overspray is dry before it lands on something you didn't want to be coated with the finish. In my shop, it just becomes another layer of inert dust in an already dust-covered environment.

Lacquer is clear, so it brings out the true colors of wood. I prefer lacquer when I want a more subtle, elegant finish.

The downside, in my experience, is that dozens of layers of lacquer are required for a good coating.

Polyurethane is a plastic-based finish. Once the polymers in the finish are exposed to air and the solvents or water (depending on if it is oil- or water-based) evaporate, polyurethane forms a plastic coating. But, once it's done, no amount of solvent is going to make it workable again. If a mistake is made, sanding or stripping is required to remove it. Polyurethane is slower drying, especially if it's done in a cool environment, but it takes fewer coats to get an attractive surface.

Since polyurethane will never liquefy again, it requires sanding in between coats so that the new coat has something to adhere to. While it doesn't require hard sanding, it is another time-consuming step. Don't get impatient. If sanding is done before the coat is dry, the coating can ball up and become gluelike. When that happens, the area needs to be sanded down past the damage and redone. The best advice is to be patient and make sure the workplace is in the temperature range specified by the maker of the finish.

Polyurethane dries to a light amber cast, which most people find to be warm and pleasant. The finish gives a plastic coating look that some feel gives the piece an unnatural look and feel.

Since polyurethane takes so long to dry, it is good for filling in slight surface imperfections, but it is very prone to flowing and dripping off edges. It is also terrible for overspray. It stays wet for long periods and is prone to adhering to anything downwind. So things like air compressor gauges, hand tools, and truck windshields can all get coated if you're not careful. Don't ask me how I know.

But, even with the negative points, polyurethane provides the most durable and popular finish on the market.

Stains

Most log furniture makers don't use stains, preferring instead to showcase the natural colors of the woods. But there are woods that are so bland that staining greatly enhances them. Black locust is one wood that comes to mind.

While most woods are beautiful naturally, staining a piece helps to bring it together visually.

Staining is also useful when a furniture maker wants all of the wood to be the same color. Even in the same species, wood can vary in color. To make a piece of furniture more uniform, a builder will stain all of it a color close to the natural color. This is especially useful when doing sets of chairs or tables.

Making Your Own Stains

If you've ever had a black walnut tree in your yard, you know how badly the hulls stain driveways, decks, and patios. That same pigment can be used to stain wood. All you need to do is soak the hulls in water for a few days to get a dark stain that is almost impossible to remove, especially when it gets on your hands.

One of the woodworking secrets is using lye on cherry wood to age it. Cherry naturally darkens as it ages, but it takes years, sometimes generations, to get a certain hue. Furniture makers often need to match older cherry furniture when making repairs. When artificial aging is required, they use common cleaning lye. The lye reacts with the wood and darkens the surface, just as if it had been cut a hundred years ago! Even if you're not trying to match existing wood, darkening cherry can make the wood more interesting and warm.

Beware: Lye is deadly if not used properly. Always apply it in a well-ventilated area, use PPE, and keep it away from children and pets.

Let a mix of vinegar and steel wool sit for a day or so, and it will produce a dye that will darken some woods like oak, cedar, and pine. The wood often changes to a weathered look that rustic furniture lovers admire.

To be honest, there are hundreds of plants that can be used as a dye. Weavers and leather makers have been using plant and bark dyes for thousands of years. In most cases, it takes a great deal of plant matter to dye wood, and the color is usually very subtle.

There are many books on the topic of plant dyes, and the Internet is a great resource to see what other people are doing and how they are doing it. If you decide to experiment, be sure to keep good notes on your recipe, otherwise you may never be able to duplicate the hue again.

Be careful. Just because the dye is natural, doesn't mean it's safe for children or pets to be around.

Once the dye or stain has dried thoroughly, you can apply the finish to preserve it just as you would with commercially made stains.

Lye ages cherry wood as if it has been in use for generations.

CHAPTER 16
PORTABLE BAND SAW MILLS

*I*f you do much log work, you'll hear about portable band saw mills like Wood-Mizer. Band saw mills are rated for the maximum-diameter log they will cut. If you have the money, they are great for cutting boards out of logs. Another great thing to cut is flitches or slabs. Slab tables are big sellers and a favorite of any rustic furniture lover. The only problem is keeping the slabs flat as they dry.

If you don't have the money or room for a portable band saw mill, don't worry. If you contact Wood-Mizer, they keep track of who owns their products and can direct you to the nearest owner. It has been my experience that band saw mill owners are very reasonable, considering the service they provide.

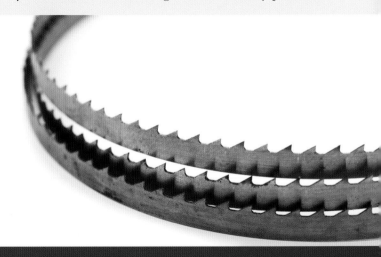

Chain Saw Lumber Mills

Yes, they make attachments for chain saws to turn them into board-cutting machines. However, before you fall for their siren song of easy lumber, heed my warning. There is nothing quick or easy about a chain saw mill.

First, a high-horsepower chain saw is required. I use a Stihl 460, which is 5 hp, and it still bogs down at times.

Second, it takes quite a bit of setup before you can make your first cut. A track has to be set up on the log for the mill to ride on. I use an old extension ladder instead of buying their expensive rail system.

Third, the chains are not cheap. I have a 28" (70 cm) bar, so I can cut 20" (50 cm) logs.

Lastly, the cuts can take forever. When cutting twelve-foot-long (4 m) cherry or hickory logs, it can take ten to fifteen minutes per cut, and that's choking on exhaust fumes and sawdust the whole time!

Chainsaw distress marks on aspen.

BUT... I have also made some of the coolest looking tables and benches from wood I have cut using my chain saw lumber mill. As I cuss and swear, working the blade back and forth, trying to make it cut faster, it imparts a "feathered" pattern that, if allowed to weather a little, collectors love.

Funny story: I brought a table with the new "feathered" pattern to a store that sold my pieces. The owner turned up her nose at it, commenting that it would never sell, but took it anyway. Within days she called me to say the table had sold, and to ask if I could make more just like it.

Tools

Tools are expensive but make the impossible possible. My recommendation is to buy the big-ticket items used. Some of my best tools have come from auctions, moving sales, and estate sales.

Dill bits

Almost all joints will require a hole. There are many styles of wood-boring drill bits on the market, but some are better suited for log furniture making than others. There are two key features that make a good drill bit. First, it needs to make a clean, straight hole. Second, the bit needs to stop cutting when YOU want it to stop.

Some of the cheapest drill bits on the market are the paddle or spade bits. They work well and are easy to sharpen. But they also have a long pilot tip that can exit the opposite side of the log if you are not careful.

Twist drills work well for screw pilot holes, but I do not recommend them for anything larger. A larger twist drill can easily grab the wood and cut too deep, ruining a piece before you can react.

Auger bits work well in construction but have no place in the furniture maker's shop. The screw tip pulls the bit through wood fast—too fast. The hole is anything but clean, and by the time the drill comes to a stop, the hole will be too deep or all the way through the piece.

The preferred drill bit for log furniture makers is the Forstner bit. They make a clean hole with a shallow pilot, and stop cutting when you stop pushing.

A full set of Forstner bits are vital to a woodworker.

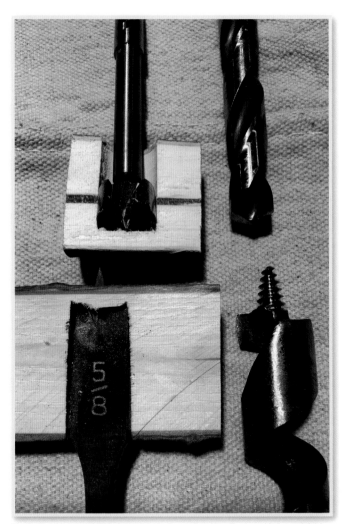

The Forstner bit (upper left) is the best choice for woodworking. The auger bit (lower right) is the worst choice. The paddle bit works well, but the pilot tip might poke an undesirable hole.

Clamps

Wood clamps are indispensable. Along with the normal board gluing/clamping function, they also can be used to draw tenons into holes, hold pieces together for making a mock-up, pushing components apart, and many other jobs. You can never have too many wood clamps of various sizes.

Larger clamps can gently persuade pieces to move when tenons are tight. They can also be used to disassemble pieces after a mock-up.

There's no such thing as too many wood clamps, especially when gluing down bark.

Drawknife

I have a drawknife. I don't use it. The only time I take it out of the drawer is to clean up a live edge on a slab. If the logs are cut and peeled in the right season, you won't need a drawknife.

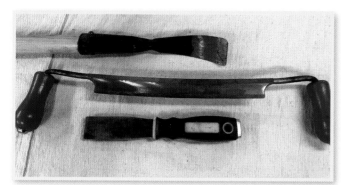

A barking spud (top); a drawknife (middle); and a used putty knife (bottom), which works better at peeling logs than the barking spud or drawknife.

Putty knife

I know a lowly putty knife isn't macho like a drawknife, but it's what I use to peel logs. A good putty knife will be your best friend when working with logs. Trust me on this.

Japanese saw

The Japanese saw is usually a flexible saw with no kerf. Due to these two attributes, woodworkers use the saw to cut dowels and tenons flush with the wood face without scratching the wood surface. They are nice when new, but one bent tooth can cause scratching.

Japanese saws do not have kerf; this allows them to trim exposed tenons without marring the mating wood.

Curved base planer

As the name implies, the base on this planer is curved, not flat. Since the base is curved, the planer follows the contour of the log very closely, making it a great tool for stripping bark from stubborn logs. The only maker available at the time I am writing this is Makita. The model number is 1002BA.

Makita's curved base planer, used for peeling logs.

Hand plane

While hand planes are a bit old-fashioned, they are just the ticket for breaking a long edge or taking off a high spot on an otherwise flat surface. Keep the blade sharp and take a shallow bite, and you'll be surprised how well an old-fashioned plane will work.

Electric planer

Planers of the electric variety really help flatten table slabs. Just be careful and only take off a little material on a pass. You also want to go with the grain. If the wood keeps chipping out, try switching directions. Some wood, like hickory, has such a crazy grain you're going to get some chipping no matter what you do.

The old hand plane and modern electric plane both have their place when making rustic furniture.

Surface planer

I would be lost without my surface planer. It takes a rough-cut board and transforms it into beautiful lumber. Keep your blades sharp, and the surface planer will be your best friend.

87

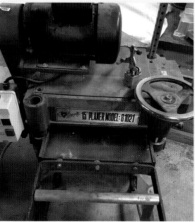

Smaller surface planers like the Dewalt (left) will do most jobs under 12" (300 mm) wide, but tough woods like hickory require a more powerful machine. The 15" (380 mm) planer (right) has a two-horsepower motor that cuts most wood like a knife through butter.

> ✓ **TIP**
>
> Many hobby models are underpowered for tough woods. Woods like hickory max out the smaller surface planer models, even at their slowest feed setting and taking a light cut. If you can afford it, buy a larger model. I have a 120-volt, fractional-horsepower, 13" (330 mm) model and a 240-volt, three-horsepower, 15" (380 mm) model. The power difference between the two is like night and day.

Jointer

Okay, don't tell the surface planer, but my jointer is also my best friend. I have a six-inch (150 mm) model that I got at an auction for twenty-five bucks, and it was the best money I have ever spent. If I want to flatten the side of a log so I can attach boards or slabs, I just run them over the jointer until I have the surface I want. The same goes for facing half logs. It makes me look like a professional in no time.

Old but built like a tank, this six-inch (150 mm) jointer was an estate auction treasure.

> ✓ **TIP**
>
> The longer the jointer bed is, the better it is at removing twists or curves in boards.

Surface grinder

Yes, this is the same grinder used by metal workers everywhere. It is also known as a right-angle grinder. I put a sanding wheel on mine to quickly sand down knots and branch stubs. I also use it to clean up rough tenons.

A surface grinder isn't just for metal. I use an aggressive sanding disk to remove knots protruding from logs and to trim legs that need leveling.

Battery drill

A high-quality ½" (13 mm) chuck battery drill is a lifesaver. I drill almost all my holes and small tenons with a battery drill.

Right-angle drill

The right-angle drill is an investment in your health. If you have ever twisted a wrist when using a drill, you know what I mean. An accident can break bones and tear tendons on wrists, fingers, or worse. The right-angle drill gives you a long handle that tames all that torque when drilling big holes or cutting tenons.

As I write this, Milwaukee and Dewalt make almost identical corded drills with a ½" (13 mm) chuck. Milwaukee's version is called the Super Hawg, model 1680-20. It is two-speed, with the low speed being 450 rpm, and it has a drill-stopping clutch in it if the torque gets too great.

Dewalt's version is the DW124. It also has two speeds, but the slow speed is at 300 rpm, making it almost perfect for use with big tenon cutters. It also has the clutch, but it also comes with a large secondary handle that can be taken off if desired. Given a choice, I would buy the Dewalt model. I may be biased, because my Dewalt DW124 has served me without one iota of trouble for a quarter of a century now.

Miter saw

The miter saw will be your right-hand man around the shop. A good twelve-inch (300 mm) model can cut fairly good-sized logs in one clean cut. They are great when cutting logs to length, squaring up the ends, or just shaving another quarter-inch (5 mm) off a tenon.

A right-angle drill is the best choice for cutting large tenons.

Logs are easy to cut perfectly with a 12" (300 mm) miter saw.

Radial arm saw

These dinosaurs from the late 20th century have fallen out of favor with woodworkers, but they actually have a use in my shop. My 1983 Sears & Roebuck Craftsman model has followed me around the country and is on its third or fourth table.

Fortunately, I bought the sander, surface planer, and ¼" (6 mm) collet attachments when they were still available. The attachments go at the end of the shaft opposite from the blade.

By pivoting the head and putting the surface planer on it, I have a wood-milling machine. I can lay a slab of hickory on the table and slowly pull the head out on its track and across the slab, milling the surface flat. By inching the board around on the table or pivoting the radial arm saw arm, I can hit the entire slab face. Just flip the slab over and do the same, and I have one flat slab that would make almost any machinist happy.

With the drum sander attachment, I have a large drum sander to work edges and convex shapes.

With the ¼" (6 mm) collet attachment, I can use any router or shaper bit with a ¼" (6 mm) shank.

If you haunt eBay, Craigslist, or the countless other classified selling websites, I am sure you could find everything you need to do the same and more.

Band saw

I could make it without my band saw, but things would be much slower. I use mine to trim up any branch nubs left on the log after rough-cleaning it. A good three- to five-tooth per inch blade works best.

Chain saw

For cutting down trees and cutting logs to length, a lightweight twelve- to eighteen-inch (300–450 mm) model is great. If you are going to be making lumber or cutting trees for a portable band saw, you'll want a little bigger model. I have a 16" (400 mm) model for smaller jobs and a 28" (700 mm) model for larger jobs.

Angle gauge

When making legs of benches and chairs, it helps to have them at a slight angle. The problem in doing so is repeating the same angle from leg to leg, and then drilling the mortises for the crosspieces correctly on a drill press.

An angle gauge takes a great deal of that frustration away. It's an inexpensive tool that pays for itself the first time you use it.

An angle gauge helps match angles on tenons.

CHAPTER 17
GLUE AND GLUING

*T*here are many different types of glue on the market. They all serve their purpose if used properly. Be sure to follow the manufacturer's recommendations on use and clamping times. In fact, double the clamping time.

Proper wood glue, like Titebond, is required for strong joints.

Wood glue

Elmer's and Titebond seem to be the two leaders in this market. They are the common yellow wood glue that is used for the majority of woodworking. If I'm joining boards to make a seat or table top, this is what I use exclusively.

CA glue

Known officially as cyanoacrylate and unofficially as super glue, most woodworkers refer to it as CA. Cyanoacrylate is extremely fast working and bonds to almost everything. It is also very thin and is perfect for repairing loose or chipped bark. Some woodworkers use it as a wood sealer, and even as a finish on small projects.

CA is a double-edge sword, as it can *cause* issues right along with fixing others. I have had it accidentally stain an otherwise beautiful tabletop. I also have never fully used

✓ TIP

Wipe off any yellow glue that squeezes out of a joint with a moist rag. Leaving it can cause a yellow tint to light wood.

an entire bottle without spilling a large portion of it or had the dispenser tip seal itself closed. Still, expensive as it is, I always have some on hand.

CA comes in different thicknesses, ranging from watery thin to jelly thick. They all can come in handy, but be sure to also have a bottle of CA de-bonder handy in case you have an accident and glue something you didn't want to.

Urethane glue

Urethane glue can be a gift from heaven or a curse from hell. Urethane glue expands as a foam as it dries, making a wiggle-free joint. But it is a struggle to dispense the correct amount of glue, and I always seem to fall on the "dispense-too-much" side. Without a doubt, urethane glue is a great bond that works wonders at filling tenon joints. But urethane glue also expands out of places where it shouldn't and makes a huge mess. If that wasn't enough of a problem, it can also stain light wood, which means more labor of sanding something I otherwise would not have to sand.

Epoxy filler

Slabs have voids in them for a multitude of reasons. If the void is undesirable, it can be filled with tinted epoxy. The process is simple but time-consuming.

First, find a way to dam the epoxy where you want it to stay. This entails blocking off the bottom of the void and any place open on the sides. Sheet metal, duct tape, and thin plywood all work. Be sure to also add a layer of tape to the wood surface around the void to protect it from unwanted epoxy.

Mix up enough epoxy to fill the void, and add the tint. Please note that epoxy tint is NOT wood stain. Woodworking outlets sell many different shades of epoxy tint. I try to match the color of the natural knots in the wood.

Pour the epoxy into the void. It has been my experience that this is a multi-stage process, because the epoxy always finds a place to ooze to that I didn't count on. Once the epoxy is level with the wood surface and hard, it can be sanded or planed like normal.

✓ BEWARE

If you overdo it with the epoxy and cover the wood around the void, it will fill the pores in the wood, causing it to have an undesirable blackhead effect.

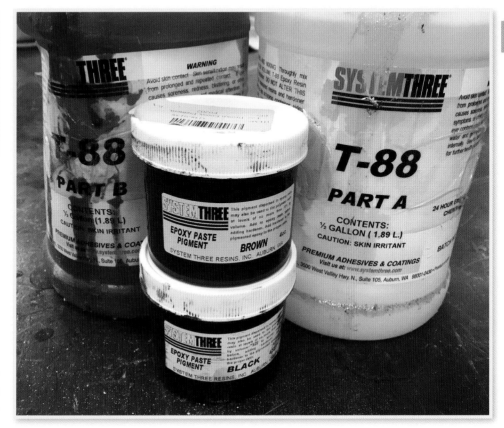

Epoxy is normally clear or amber-colored, but it can be tinted to match the surrounding wood.

91

CHAPTER 18
SANDING

I don't care how perfect a planed surface looks, I always sand it down before applying a finish. I have yet to see a planer blade that didn't leave marks that need to be removed by sanding. The way to sand is to use a coarse grit to remove any planer marks and imperfections, then use progressively finer grit to remove any sanding marks left by the previous step. For me, this usually means starting out with 80 grit and working my way up to 220 or 320 grit. If the surface is really damaged, I might start with 40 grit.

A random orbit sander (front) is required equipment for a smooth surface. Use a belt sander with caution, as they can quickly cause damage to wood that will be almost impossible to repair.

The Good, the Bad, and the Ugly of Sanding

The choice of a sander is critical to the end product.

The Good: Random orbit sanders are currently the best way to sand, in my humble opinion. Since they are a random orbit, they do not leave a sanding pattern in the wood. Models these days also have quick-change options for the sandpaper. I personally like the hook and loop system.

The Bad: Orbital and ¼ sheet sanders were a huge step up from belt sanders, but in the wrong hands, they still cause problems. They both used a nonrandom movement that could quickly cause hard-to-remove sanding marks.

The Ugly: Years ago, belt sanders were all the rage. I have one. I don't use it often. They are great at removing material fast— often, too fast. They are meant to be used by sanding with the grain, but even then a belt sander can quickly cause more problems than it was supposed to fix. In the wrong hands, a belt sander can burn or gouge a board. It can easily cause hills and valleys on larger surfaces. And heaven forbid you decide to sand across the grain. Good luck getting the marks out.

CHAPTER 19
WORKSTATIONS

Good USA wood vises are hard to find, but yard sales and flea markets can turn up treasures.

✓ TIP

Your workstations need to be the correct height for you. A good rule of thumb is to have the work surface the same height as your thumb knuckle as it hangs at your side.

There's a reason lumberjacks are burly folks with bulging muscles in flannel shirts; green logs are heavy. Don't believe me? A fresh-cut pine or aspen log that averages 5" (125 mm) in diameter runs roughly thirty-seven pounds (16.8 kg) for every 6' (1.8 m) of length. Ash logs of the same dimensions average around fifty-six pounds (25.4 kg), hickory around sixty-three pounds (28.6 kg).

Are you thinking about hauling a log out of the woods? You better have the right equipment because a 20" (0.5 m) hickory that's 8' (2.4 m) long is roughly thirteen hundred pounds (590 kg)!

There are two points I need to make. First, do as much of the work of peeling, cleaning, and prepping the logs before you move them. The more weight that is removed from a log, the easier it is on you and your equipment. Second, make sure your workstations can stand up to the task that you're asking them to do. This isn't the time or place to buy a cheap, sheet-metal workbench or rinky-dink plastic saw horses.

The logs are already heavy. Add the kinetic energy of a log as it's jostled about and the motions of peeling, cutting, scraping, and drilling, and there's huge potential for an accident. Making log furniture can be exciting, and can lead to cutting corners in order to get going, but take the time to make sure your workstations can handle the abuse.

Peeling logs

I strongly recommend peeling your logs in the woods if at all possible. This does two things: It keeps the mess in the woods where you don't have to clean it up, and as the bark rots away the nutrients go right back where nature intended.

The sawbuck

When peeling and cleaning logs, few things help more than a sawbuck. It is nothing more than two Xs strung together to make a cradle to hold logs at a proper working height that isn't going to kill your back. You can make it fancy from pipe or simple from lumber. Not only does it save your back, it keeps the log from rolling around in the dirt as you strip it.

The key to it all: the workbench

Your workbench is key to being able to work without frustration and back pain. The workbench needs to be large enough to hold a headboard, strong enough to support cutting logs, and level enough to check the trueness of your furniture legs.

My workbench is a wooden, commercial, solid-core door that I rescued from a construction dumpster. It is perfectly flat and heavy enough to take almost any abuse I throw on it. The frame I built for it keeps the top from flexing or wiggling. It is as solid as the Rock of Gibraltar.

My workbench is also where I have my wood vise attached. My wood vise is my tenon cutting station, so the workbench has to be heavy enough to absorb the torque of the tenon cutter and drill without moving. The height is perfect for me and minimizes the need for me to lean over my work.

A good, sturdy workbench is the center of any workshop. This is a recycled solid-core door.

95

CHAPTER 20

THE BASICS OF
MAKING FURNITURE

*J*f you really want basic, think back to a camping trip. Sometime in your past, you most likely sat on a log lying on its side next to a campfire. That was a simple bench. Possibly, on that same adventure, you turned a cut log on end to use as a chair or table. Simple, yes, but they got the job done. Log furniture can be that simple and still have a place in an elegant home.

The edge of this table is not a live edge, but it is so well done that few would care.

A table can be as simple as a section of log that has been sanded smooth and finished.

Tables, chairs, benches, and other similar furniture all have a few things in common. They have a flat, level surface to place things on. They have legs that support the flat surface at a specified height. It's that simple.

Most furniture has four legs, but the piece can be as simple as a section of a log stood on end, or as complex as a tangle of roots or gnarly wood.

Most furniture is made to accepted industry norms, meaning most furniture is built to a height, width, and depth that people have come to expect.

Most dining room tables are 30" (75 cm) tall, 30" (75 cm) wide, and 42" (1 m) long.

Most end tables are 24" (60 cm) tall, 18" (45 cm) wide, and 24" (60 cm) deep.

Most coffee tables are 18" (45 cm) tall, 18–24" (45–60 cm) wide, and 48–60" (1.2–1.5 m) long.

Most hall tables are 30" (75 cm) tall, 16" (40 cm) wide, and 30–50" (75–125 cm) long.

If you don't build to accepted standards, the piece may be a hard sell. That's not to say you can't be creative and make something unique, as long as it fulfills the purpose it was made for.

As you are planning a piece of furniture and gathering wood, visualize how the piece is going to work. How thick is the top going to be? How wide and long is the top going to be? How long do the legs need to be? How are the legs going to attach to the top? How is the top going to be held together? Is it going to be one solid piece, pieces joined together with no seams, or planks laid side by side? How are you going to brace the legs to keep the piece from being wobbly? These are all things that you need to think of before you cut the first piece.

If you don't know what you want to do, go to a furniture store or go online and see how a similar piece is made, then visualize how you can do it with logs and rustic materials.

As you plan, think of how you are going to make the cuts, make the flat surfaces, make the joints, and so on and so forth. Often, we're limited by the capabilities of our tools, our skills, and our time.

As an example, I was making a coffee table out of a slab cut from a large hickory. The slab was roughly 24" (60 cm) wide by 60" (1.5 m) long, far too big for any surfacing tool I have. To plane hard hickory down by hand would take an immense amount of labor. As I studied the slab, I realized that if I cut the slab down the center, the two halves would be narrow enough to go through my electric surface planer. By being careful in my cut, all I had to do was run the two mating edges through my jointer a couple of times. Using a biscuit jointer, the slab top glued back together perfectly, and the whole process was easy and quick. Most individuals can't tell the slab was ever split, unless I point out the seam.

97

A Word on Slabs and Lumber

Actually, we need to go over the other words used to describe slabs and rough-cut lumber because it can get confusing and the meaning can change from sawyer to sawyer.

Waney edge/live edge

As a tree is cut into slabs, the sawyer often just takes longitudinal slices off the original log, allowing the edges of the slab to be the actual outside of the tree. In most cases, buyers desire this natural look.

False fronts

Many buyers desire the live edge look, but sometimes it's hard to achieve the perfect look without getting creative. Some furniture makers use pieces of bark fastened on to give the live edge look. Other builders use sawmill discards to use as drawer faces or the edges of tables. I have done something similar by cutting smaller cedar logs into quarters and piecing them together to make an attractive false front on drawers.

The gentle curve of the front of this table is a live edge.

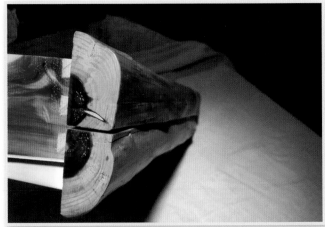

The front of this drawer is actually two sections cut from cedar logs to provide a larger, natural log face.

The live outside edges of this table are actually mating pieces from a crotch of a hickory.

The branches do nothing to strengthen the piece, but they do add character.

Flitch

A longitudinal piece of wood cut from a tree with both live edges present is referred to as a flitch. But it can also refer to a beam made from separate pieces of lumber, or even a slab of bacon!

Slab

In general, a slab is a thick section of wood. It can have cut edges or live edges, or both.

Native lumber

If you ever do any reclaimed lumber work, you may run into what is referred to as "native lumber." In generations past, our ancestors didn't have a home improvement center where they could buy supplies. If they wanted to build a house or barn, they needed to find a local sawmill to buy lumber or have their own logs cut into lumber. They didn't care what species the wood was, as long as they could put a roof over their heads and keep the wind out. In the eastern U.S., this often meant oak and walnut were used right along with poplar and beech. Almost always the lumber was left rough-cut because they didn't care. A coating of lathe and plaster made them all look the same anyway.

As I said elsewhere in this book, always be on the watch for valuable wood when dealing with reclaimed native lumber, especially on old barns.

Bracing

Installing braces, gussets, and cross-members adds to the strength of a piece and stops a piece from swaying and rocking. They can also add to the look of the piece. I strongly recommend using them whenever possible.

A WORD ON LUMBER DIMENSIONING

At any U.S. retailer other than a home improvement store, lumber thickness is referred to in fourths of an inch. So, an inch-thick board is referred to as being ⁴⁄₄ths. A two-inch board is referred to as ⁸⁄₄ths.

In the woodworking world, much of the wood is sold "rough cut." All this means is that the wood is just as it came off the saw. No finishing has been done. If you've ever bought a two by four (50 x 100 mm) at a home improvement store, you will notice it really isn't two inches by four inches. That's because the wood has been planed smooth and sometimes even sanded. The finishing process removed material, making the dimensions smaller in the process, so a 2" by 4" (50 x 100 mm) board ends up being 1.5" by 3.5" (45 x 90 mm).

Bracing strengthens a piece while adding visual interest.

99

The arches on this hall table were carefully steam bent. They strengthen the piece while adding elegance.

PART 2

BUILDING THE FURNITURE

CHAPTER 21

BUILDING A SLAB BENCH

Version One

A slab bench is as basic a piece of furniture as you can get. Start with a strong, thick plank or slab.

Using a Forstner bit, drill the holes, known as a mortise, for the leg tenons. I drill mine at a slight angle and use a 1 ½" (35 mm) bit. Why angle the legs? The wider the stance of the legs, the more stable it is.

If you decide to drill all the way through the bench, that's fine. The exposed tenon face will add extra character to the piece. But keep in mind, it will require more work to make it look nice.

Cut four legs of equal diameter and length. Benches should be about 18" (450 mm) to the top, so the legs will need to be slightly longer than 18" (450 mm) because they will be at an angle.

Cut a tenon on each leg and insert them in the mortises on the bench. Fasten each leg to the bench. I like to use screws at an angle.

Flip the bench over and correct any leg that's too high and makes the bench wobble. Sand and finish.

Version Two

This version of a log slab bench is a little more complex, yet is also more appealing to many folks. It also requires the use of a radial arm saw to make the dados.

Start with a nice slab. Many benches are 48" (1.2 m) long and 12" (300 mm) wide. In this style, the sides are cut off to provide a flat surface. A circular saw works well for this.

Once the slab is the size required, measure in four inches (100 mm) for the dados that the cross pieces will rest in. Cut the dado two inches (50 mm) wide. The thickness of the remaining slab can vary but this was made two inches (50 mm).

Next cut two crosspieces roughly six inches (150 mm) longer than the bench is wide, to allow making the tenons. If you would like a smooth mating surface, run the two crosspieces through a jointer to give them a level strip to mate the dado cut.

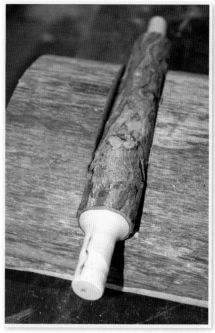

A crosspiece with tenons is carefully fit into the dado.

A dado is cut using a radial arm saw.

Cut the tenons, taking care not to cut them too far.

Cut four 18" (450 mm) legs. With the crosspieces lying in the dado cuts, line up the legs next to the tenons and mark where the tenon holes need to be.

Drill the tenon holes to match the crosspieces. If the crosspieces are too long to allow the leg to fit up tight to the slab, trim the crosspiece tenon until it does.

Once the legs fit correctly, measure and cut brace tenon holes and brace crosspieces. Fit them together to match the upper crosspieces.

Assemble the crosspieces and legs together, and when everything looks correct, screw and pin the pieces.

Mortises are marked and drilled on each leg.

The legs and struts are added as the bench is assembled.

The finished bench is beautiful and sturdy.

With the legs attached to the bench top, cut and fasten cross braces to prevent wobble. Fastening the two braces together where they cross adds strength and rigidity.

CHAPTER 22

MAKING A RUSTIC FRAMED MIRROR

Birch bark frames are a Northwoods classic. Unfortunately, we don't have any native white birch in Indiana. I procured a small supply of bark on a hunting trip up north. The resort I was staying at had a dead birch. With their permission, I stripped off all that I thought I would need. After starting to work with it, I wished I had cut more. Let that be a lesson.

A common feature on birch bark is the lenticels, which is a fancy name for the black dash marks. I wanted my twigs to have matching lenticels. Not having the time or funds to make another material-gathering trip up north, I chose to use black cherry branches, which also have the same classic lenticels and can easily stand in for birch twigs.

While it may seem to be a crime to cut down valuable future black cherry saplings, they grow like weeds around my place. In fact, they are a great candidate for coppicing.

MATERIALS REQUIRED

- ✓ 20" (500 mm) by 24" (600 mm) glass mirror

- ✓ (2) Pine boards—finished dimensions 29" (750 mm) long, 5" (125 mm) wide, ¾" (20 mm) thick

- ✓ (2) Pine boards—finished dimensions 33" (850 mm) long, 5" (125 mm) wide, ¾" (20 mm) thick

- ✓ A supply of birch bark long enough and wide enough to cover the frame

- ✓ A supply of various-thickness twigs to cover the edges and seams

The frame was made from common pine, then spray painted flat black so that the frame is harder to see under the twigs.

Birch bark rarely lies perfectly flat and has to be persuaded by wood clamps.

107

1. Cut the boards to the length and width desired.

2. Rabbet one edge of each board using a router. The cut should be ⅜" (10 mm) by ½" (12 mm) to provide a pocket for the mirror.

3. Miter the corners to produce a frame with a 20" (500 mm) by 24" (600 mm) pocket.

4. Glue the frame together and brace the miter joints with ¼" (6 mm) thick plywood pieces or metal straps.

5. Paint the outer and inner edges of the frame black.

6. Glue the birch bark to the frame surface and clamp well.

7. Trim bark flush with the frame.

8. Touch up black paint if required.

9. Install a piece of plywood in the frame as if it were the mirror. The plywood keeps you from accidentally installing twigs too deep.

10. Cover the inner and outer frame edges with twigs. Start with larger twigs and use smaller twigs to cover any gaps. An 18-gauge nail gun is very helpful in this step.

11. Cut larger twigs in two and use them to cover the bark seams.

12. Remove the plywood panel.

13. Install the mirror and fasten in place.

14. Install a frame-hanging kit.

Note that all of my birch bark pieces have the lenticels horizontal as if I peeled the entire frame from the tree in one piece.

The edges and bark seams are covered with black cherry suckers. The effect is rustic elegance.

CHAPTER 23

RUSTIC COAT RACK

The biggest problem when designing a coat rack is to ensure that it will not fall over under normal use. The two key points: Make the base wide enough or heavy enough to lower the center of gravity, and design the coat hooks long enough to hold a heavy coat, yet close enough to keep the load in the center.

The key components for a coat rack are the pole, the base, and the coat hooks.

There are many ways to build a base, and most work if they are made right. I prefer a pinwheel-pattern base made from four boards. I add 12" (300 mm) to the diameter of the pole base to get the board length. In the example shown, the base is 2½" (60 mm) in diameter, so the side of the base is 14½" (350 mm). The center square is just large enough to accept the pole snugly. The legs are going to be under a great deal of stress, so glue and screw them together.

Next is to add the struts to stabilize the pole. I use simple smaller sapling pieces and fasten them to the pole and the base. They stabilize the base and keep it from becoming loose and leaning. Use a level to make sure the pole is as close to perpendicular as possible.

The base is reclaimed walnut native lumber. The joints were glued and screwed together.

Struts are added for stability and strength.

111

The last thing to add is the coat hooks. I prefer to use natural hooks created when the main stem of a sapling becomes stunted or dies out. A branch often takes over as the main stem as the tree reaches for the sun. These branches make strong, natural hooks that look better, in my opinion, than manufactured pegs.

If you can't find natural hooks, don't despair. Many builders use short sections of saplings and tenon them into the main pole. For a rustic, Western feel, builders use old horseshoes as the hooks. If you want to be really lazy, shaker pegs can be bought at almost any home builder's store or hobby center.

The coat rack is ready for polyurethane.

A session in the woods produced bent hickory limbs that were cut into matching pairs of coat hooks.

Add the coat hooks to the stand with sturdy countersunk screws.

Making a Wall-Mounted Coat Rack

Sometimes a wall-mounted coat rack is better than a free-standing model. They are also easier to make.

Shown are two examples. One is made from a sassafras log half that has hickory pegs installed. The other is reclaimed lumber from an old barn and old horseshoes. I used a torch to heat the horseshoes and bent them in a vise while still red hot.

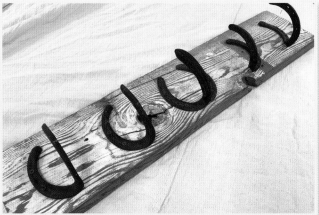

The log sections were left over from another project. The wood was too pretty just to throw back into the woods, so I added hickory pegs and repurposed them as wall-mounted coat racks. It was a good play because they sold instantly.

This wall-mounted coat rack started life as part of a barn and horseshoes.

Keep your eyes open at shops and you'll see other ways to make coat racks.

113

CHAPTER 24

MAKING TABLES

All tables have a few things in common. They all have four legs. They all have a top. They all have to be stable and strong enough to perform the task for which they were intended. The only differences between tables are the dimensions of the top and the height that they stand.

There are industry guidelines for tables. I recommend adhering to them closely, especially in height.

TABLES	HEIGHT	WIDTH	LENGTH
Bedside	26" (65 cm)	15" (38 cm)	19" (48 cm)
Coffee	19" (48 cm)	18" (45 cm)	48" (1.2 m)
Conference	30" (75 cm)	36" (90 cm)	96" (2.4 m)
Dining	29" (73 cm)	40" (1 m)	64" (1.6 m)
End	20" (50 cm)	18" (45 cm)	28" (70 cm)
Hall	27" (68 cm)	15" (38 cm)	55" (1.4 m)
Kitchen	29" (73 cm)	36" (90 cm)	60" (1.5 m)
Poker	29" (73 cm)	48" (1.2 m)	48" (1.2 m)
Sofa	26" (65 cm)	14" (35 cm)	72" (1.8 m)

In my opinion, the easiest way to make a table of any kind is to use planks or slabs. I used to join the top boards together to make one solid top, but in the dog-eat-dog world of making log furniture, that takes too much time and effort. With rare exceptions, I now use planks to make up the top and leave a small gap between the boards.

The first step in building any table is to find planks long and wide enough to make up the top, and logs of the proper size for the legs. Smaller logs or saplings will also be required for struts and braces.

I always start my tables by matching planks or slabs together that will be wide enough and long enough for the project. It's always a good idea to make a mock-up of the tabletop by arranging the boards on a bench as if it were the table. I flip and move the planks around until I'm happy with how they look.

Once the top mock-up looks good, find suitable logs to become the base to which the top is fastened. The base logs need to be large enough to allow mortises for the legs. To make the matter easier, run the base logs through a jointer to flatten one side. The flat side will provide a flat surface to fasten the top planks to.

Running the crosspieces over a jointer provides a smooth, level starting surface.

Once you have the base logs flattened, place them on the tabletop to figure your spacing for screws with which to attach the top and for proper length. I like the log ends to be visible but not sticking out past the top. If everything looks great, drill the mortises for the legs.

In my example, I drilled the mortises all the way through the base. I then change to my bevel bit and set my drill press stop so that the bevel stops at the same spot for each mortise. In this manner, each mortise is the same depth, and each tenon can be the same length.

Drill and countersink the mortises for the legs. By setting the drill press stops in place on the countersink cuts and setting the tenon stops, each leg and matching mortise will be almost identical.

Once the mortises are drilled, I drill pilot holes for the screws that will hold the base to the top planks. Plan on at least two screws per plank, per side.

When all the pilot holes are done, fasten the base logs to the top planks, making sure the screws are long enough to get a good bite, yet short enough to not go all the way through the top.

Now that the top is one solid piece, lay it face down on the workbench with something under it to protect it from damage. A sheet of cardboard works well.

Take your legs and cut the tenons to match the depth of the mortises. If you set your drill press correctly, they should all be the same length. If not, don't worry about it because you can correct it later.

Once the legs have their tenons cut, stick them in the mortises, like a dead horse with its legs sticking in the air. Measure from the workbench top up and mark your cuts so that the finished tabletop will be the right height from the floor. Cut the legs and stick them back in the mortises.

At this point, you could say you're done and just fasten the legs into the mortises, but the table would most likely be wobbly, so I recommend crosspieces to add style and stability. Here's where it gets fun. When I say fun, I mean tedious. You are going to be removing and reinserting the legs over and over again as you fit crosspieces and trim work in place.

To add crosspieces and trim pieces, find smaller-diameter logs or saplings. I like crosspieces to be about one inch (25 mm) in diameter, but use what looks good to your eye. At it's most basic, you're making tiny ladders and inserting them into matching mortises. As the trim and crosspieces get smaller, so do the tenon cutters. The smallest that I like to use is five-eights of an inch (16 mm), but they go even smaller.

Remain patient as you fit pieces in, because as you work your way around the table, you're going to be carefully pulling apart joints you already made, until all the crosspieces and trim work is complete and ready to install together as one.

If you don't want to use mortise and tenons, there's no reason you can't screw the crosspieces in place on the outside or inside of the legs. It's

your table; do what you want to do. If you decide you don't like it, do it differently next time.

Once everything is fitted together, screw and pin all the pieces in place. I place my screws and pins in locations that can't be seen on casual observation.

Before anything is fastened, struts and decorative pieces need to be fit into place.

Once all pieces are fit into place, the pins and screws can be installed.

Now the table should be ready to flip over and check. You're probably going to find that it wobbles slightly. If it does, you can fix it by only using the table on thick carpeting.

I'm kidding. You really can fix it. You should notice that two of the legs never leave the workbench as you slowly wobble the table back and forth. One of those two legs that never leave the workbench surface is too long.

Using a tape measure, check the distance from the workbench surface to the top of the table. One leg is going to be slightly longer than the other. That's the one you need to shorten.

Here's what I do. I mark the long leg with string or ribbon so I won't get confused, and flip the table over so that it's lying on its top again. Take a rasp or grinder and take a little off the tip of the leg that is too long—you know, the one with the ribbon you tied to it so that you're not cutting the leg that was already short.

Just take a little off and flip the table back right again. The wobble should be less and maybe even gone. Keep doing this until you're happy with the amount of wobble.

That's it. The table is done except for applying the finish.

These tables were built using the same technique described.

Smaller-slab tables don't require crosspieces to strengthen the top. The tenons fit into blind mortises in the slab top itself.

If you want to make a smaller, simpler table, find a thick slab of wood and drill four mortises in it for legs. Cut four legs and stick them in the mortises. Add bracing and crosspieces as needed for style and stability. Bang, it's done.

Chairs are a little complex for beginners, but if you're feeling adventuresome, there are standard dimensions for various chairs. They're basically tables that people sit on.

CHAIRS	SEAT WIDTH	SEAT DEPTH	SEAT HEIGHT	SEAT BACK HEIGHT
Barstool	17" (43 cm)	17" (43 cm)	30" (75 cm)	42" (1.05 m)
Dining, Side	19" (48 cm)	19" (48 cm)	18" (45 cm)	36" (90 cm)
Dining, Arm	24" (60 cm)	18" (45 cm)	18" (45 cm)	36" (90 cm)
Easy	25" (63 cm)	26" (65 cm)	17" (43 cm)	31" (78 cm)
Kitchen	19" (48 cm)	19" (48 cm)	19" (48 cm)	34" (86 cm)
Kitchen Stool	12" (30 cm)	12" (30 cm)	27" (68 cm)	
Rocker	20" (50 cm)	26" (65 cm)	16" (40 cm)	42" (1.05 m)
Upholstered	30" (75 cm)	26" (65 cm)	16" (40 cm)	40" (1 m)

Far left: A stool uses the same angles and features of a chair. The seat on this is just plywood, foam, and vinyl.

Left: Making this chair requires a few steam bends and upholstery work.

CHAPTER 25

RUSTIC AND LOG LAMPS

Nothing accents a look better than a well-designed rustic lamp. They are a great way to use odd, unique, or found items. Beaver-cut wood, driftwood, antler rubs, vine-damaged pieces, storm-damaged pieces, and other natural gifts all make great lamps.

The key factor to a good lamp is this:

Safety—For litigation purposes, I am not going into the actual wiring of a lamp, but be aware there is a right and wrong way to wire a lamp safely. Make sure you have the correct polarity on the shell of the lamp holder. Do your research and don't make a shock hazard.

Under the same heading is making sure it's not going to be a fire hazard. All wire terminations need to be in an approved, fire-resistant box or holder. Splices, screw terminals, or other connections need to be encased in something other than wood. Ideally, the lamp cord should travel unbroken from the UL-approved (Kitemarked) plug into the UL-approved (Kitemarked) lamp holder.

Observe the proper polarity when wiring the lamp. The neutral wire goes to the silver terminal. The hot wire goes to the gold terminal.

A "UL" knot keeps the lamp cord from being pulled out of the lamp holder.

Make sure nothing will pinch, abrade, or otherwise damage the lamp cord with normal use. The safest way to achieve this is to use the threaded pipe specifically made for lights. Any hardware store or do-it-yourself center will sell the pipe as well as the lamp parts.

In my example, I drilled upward from the base of the lamp to create a void. I then drilled down from the top of the lamp into the void with a drill bit slightly bigger than the pipe, which usually is ⅜" (10 mm) O.D. From that point, it's a simple process of inserting a pipe through the hole and locking it in place with lock washers and nuts made for the job.

Do-it-yourself centers have a wide selection of lamp parts.

The lamp tubing fits snugly into the exposed hole.

By hollowing out the lamp base, the maker can insert tools to tighten the tubing nuts.

If the lamp is going to be sitting on a table, drill another hole sideways into the void in the base. This allows the lamp cord to enter the void without being pinched by the weight of the lamp.

Route the lamp cord up through the pipe and assemble the lamp fixture. That's all there is to it.

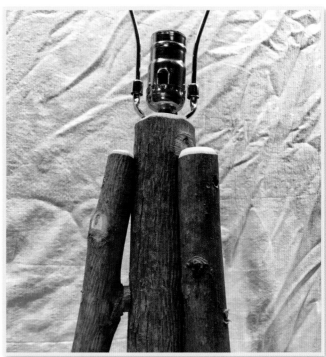

The finished lamp is ready for polyurethane.

Log lamps are common in lodges.

CHAPTER 26

BUILDING A QUILT OR RUG LADDER

In the Southwest, this is called a kiva ladder. A kiva is an underground ceremonial chamber used by the Hopi, Zuni, and other Pueblo tribes, and it requires a ladder to get in and out. Kivas and their ladders go back into history a thousand years or more.

For reasons lost to antiquity, some salesman started referring to the decorative ladders being sold in tourist stores as kiva ladders. I like the sound of the word "kiva," so I don't argue.

In most Southwestern applications, a kiva ladder is used to show off expensive Navajo rugs, or even their not so expensive knock-off copies made in Mexico and abroad.

In the Midwest, they're called quilt ladders. I can see why, since quilts are so popular in farm country and there isn't a kiva within 1,700 miles. Anyways, folks in the Midwest use them to show off expensive Amish quilts. Do you see a pattern here?

To build a ladder is easy. It requires two rails of a length that the ladder needs to be, and rungs as wide as you want, without getting ridiculous. I like to make my ladders seven to eight feet (2.1–2.4 m) tall and 18" to 24" (45–60 cm) wide.

Real ladders have a rung every foot, so that's how I make mine. Starting a foot (30 cm) from the bottom of the ladder rail, I drill a mortise every foot (30 cm), stopping a foot (30 cm) from the top. I drill matching mortises in the matching rail.

A kiva ladder is simple to make and prepares a woodworker for making headboards for beds. This one was made from tulip poplar.

It's easiest to cut a bottom rung and a top rung and fit them in without fastening. At that point, the rest of the rungs can be measured and cut. With luck, all that is required is to pull the ladder back apart, insert all the rungs, and fasten the ladder together. If it appeals to you or your client, you can even tack on a fake lashing of manila rope at each rung, just to make it look old and rustic.

BUILDING BEDS

Headboards and full beds are extremely popular with log furniture lovers, but they take a lot of logs to make.

Before I make a cut, I plan it all out. I work hard to make sure my posts and rails match in diameter and in looks. Buyers like furniture to be symmetrical. Imagine a team of horses in a parade prancing down the street: one is a draft horse, one is a Shetland pony. Would they get attention? Yes. Would they please the eye like a matched team of identical horses would? No. Symmetry is pleasing to the eye.

If I can't get all my spindles to be the same size, I at least arrange them in a manner that is pleasing to the eye, such as thinner on the outside and thicker in the center of the headboard.

I even go so far as to swap the rails end for end to try to keep the length of the spindles the same from one end to the other. (All logs have an end that is smaller than the other.) If I didn't do this step, the end that has the thicker diameter of rails would have shorter spindles than the end that has smaller diameter rails.

I design my headboards with comfort in mind. Nobody likes his or her pillow to slide off the front of the bed in the middle of the night. To stop this from happening, I place my bottom rail even with the top of the mattress. This height varies from bed to bed and also depends on the thickness of the mattress set.

In our example, let's say the top of the mattress is at 28" (70 cm). That will be the centerline of our bottom rail.

Next, decide how long you want the spindles to be. I like them to be 18" to 20" (45–50 cm) long and fit into the rails to the centerline or deeper. That places our top rail at 46" to 48" (117–122 cm) to center. I like to add a few

Beds require a great deal of material. This pile will make ONE queen-sized bed.

more inches to the posts, so let's say the posts are 52" to 54" (1.3–1.35 m) long.

Bed widths vary from size to size. Queen beds are the most popular in the U.S. and use a 60" (1.5 m) wide mattress. The mattress rails need to be outside the mattress so that the box spring can sit down into the side rails. (U.K. king size beds are roughly the same size. Measure your mattress and and make the mattress rails a little wider for the box spring.) In our example, the rails attach to the center of the posts. This means the rails need to have 60" (1.5 m) between them or roughly 62" (1.57 m) center to center of the side rails.

Our headboard and footboard rails need to be long enough to allow for this, so on a queen bed I like to cut the log rails 64" (1.6 m) long.

Keep in mind, it's always easier to trim some wood off than it is to add it back on. Try as I may, I have never been able to find a wood stretcher.

So, these are our starting dimensions:

✔ The log posts for the headboard are 52" (1.3 m) to 54" (1.35 m) long.

✔ The log rails for the headboard are 64" (1.6 m) long.

✔ The spindles are 20" (500 mm) long.

Next, figure out the spacing between the spindles. I like them 6" (150 mm) on center. Your spacing depends on your eye. What do you want them to be? I made a bed that had 12" (300 mm) between spindles. The owner loves it. It's all subjective, as long as the pillow stays on the bed.

If your bed is supposed to support the mattress, cross boards will be needed. They rest on the inside of the rail.

Chapter 27: Building Beds

A queen or king headboard and footboard require many small- to medium-diameter spindles if 6" (150 mm) spacing is used. If larger spindles are used, the spacing between them can be greater.

At this point, make a mock-up of the bed and see how you like it. Is the spacing pleasing to the eye? Is the wood symmetrical? Is everything the right length? If yes, start drilling mortises and cutting tenons.

The footboard process is the same, but I like the bottom rail to be at 12" (300 mm) off the floor, which makes the top rail 32" (800 mm) off the floor and makes the posts 36" (900 mm) tall. Your design may be different.

These twisted spindles are the center piece of the headboard.

Performing a mock-up of the piece helps avoid problems later on.

FROM TREE TO TABLE

The side rails are another matter. Beds vary in length, just as they vary in width, and mattresses can be bought in a range of depths. Here are some standard dimensions for U.S. mattresses as a rough guide.

MATTRESSES	HEIGHT	WIDTH	LENGTH
Twin (Regular)	6"	39"	75"
Twin (Long)	6"	39"	80"
Double/Full	8"	54"	75"
Queen	8"	60"	80"
King	10"	80"	80"
King (Calif.)	10"	72"	84"

Since our example is a queen bed, our rails need to be long enough to hold an 80" mattress with a little room for a comforter.

Sturdy side rails support the mattress and occupants, as well as keep the headboard and footboard locked together. Build them well.

I use 6" (150 mm) wide by 1" (25 mm) thick oak as my bed rails and add another 2" (50 mm) by 1" (25 mm) oak rib inside to place the box spring support boards on. I haven't had one break yet.

In actuality, you don't need side rails or a footboard. Many folks use just a headboard mounted to a standard steel frame. You could even mount the headboard to the wall like hotels do and not even attach it to the bed. This allows the bed to be moved easily for cleaning.

The finished queen-sized bed.

133

Book-Sawing Bed Spindles

An important piece of rustic and log furniture is natural beauty and character in the wood. In some wood species, the interior heartwood is much more interesting than the exterior sapwood.

All trees have sapwood and heartwood. To understand this, we need to realize that trees grow larger by adding a new layer of sapwood each year, just under the bark. If you read the section on removing bark from logs, you will remember that as the new layer of wood is being formed, the bark is easy to remove.

As the tree grows, the older inner wood dies, becomes denser, and darkens to some extent. The transition from sapwood to heartwood is easy to see on trees such as walnut, cherry, and cedar. The pale sapwood surrounds the darker heartwood. In traditional furniture, the bland-looking sapwood is never used in favor of the beautiful heartwood.

In log furniture, especially on tabletops, the sapwood and heartwood are used together to create a rich visual texture. But in the rest of the log furniture, the heartwood is usually only seen when the log ends are exposed. This should be a crime.

In many cases, such as chair backs or bed headboards and footboards, the spindles can be made from logs that are split or "book sawn." When a piece of wood is book sawn, the result is two pieces of wood that match grain and coloring identically. This is done a great deal on expensive traditional furniture and musical instruments. We can achieve the same thing on log furniture and make a drastically more beautiful piece.

A good candidate for this technique is red cedar or its cousin, western juniper. The exterior of cedar is already interesting to look at, but when cut in two the beautiful red heartwood is exposed.

Smaller logs can carefully be cut in two with a table saw. Larger logs will require a heavy-duty bandsaw with a sharp blade.

Once the log is cut in two, it is easy to rough cut the tenons with a bandsaw and then finish them with a tenon cutter.

Another benefit to using this technique is that two spindles can be made from each log section, thereby decreasing the total amount of wood required for a project.

The heartwood is much more stunning than the log exterior.

Trim up the end so that the tenon cutter starts in the proper location easily.

Book-sawn wood matches perfectly and saves on logs.

CHAPTER 28
TIPS, TRICKS, AND TECHNIQUES

*O*ne of the problems with passing on information to a friend is that you always remember one last tip or point you wanted to make before they go. That's what this section is: things I remembered as this book was finishing up that just didn't seem to fit anywhere else.

Imagine that we spent the day together making your first piece of furniture and now you're trying to pull out of the driveway to get home to supper. Imagine I keep waving you back to tell you one more important thing. That's what we have here, a few last things before we part ways . . .

Swiss Work

Swiss work is more a technique than a style. It encompasses placing sections of twigs, with the bark on, side by side to form a pattern or trim. In most cases I have seen, birch twigs are used, but other twigs such as hickory or black cherry can be used. I suppose you could do the same thing with saguaro cactus ribs.

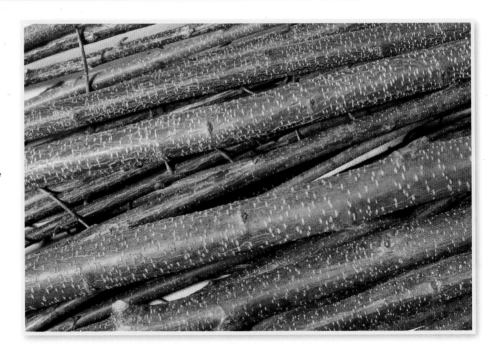

Suckers and twigs, like these black cherry suckers, are perfect for Swiss work and twig work.

Twig Work

Twig work is an art itself to get things to fit and look appealing. It is usually used with larger logs, which make a rich visual tapestry. Basically, twig work is working with small branches and twigs—extremely small twigs in some cases.

Much of twig work is used to produce a lattice or screen, which can be used on a headboard, stair rails, or similar. It is extremely tedious work, but beautiful when done correctly.

Black cherry twigs look almost identical to birch twigs.

Antler Use

Deer and elk antlers lend themselves to rustic furniture. They can be used whole as a means to make something ordinary special or add accent, or as something utilitarian like a drawer pull. If you haunt flea markets, you can find antlers for sale, or you can find them by "shed hunting" in early spring. Deer and elk shed their antlers in January and February in preparation of growing new antlers. It is a hobby of some folks to go search through the woods for these gifts of nature. Be aware that shed collecting is not allowed in national parks and other similar areas. If in doubt, ask before picking one up.

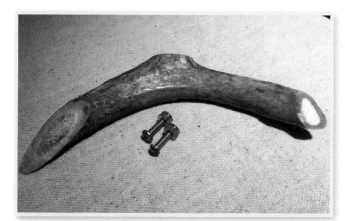

Shotshell Drawer Pulls

The base of a spent "high brass" shotgun shell makes a great drawer pull. CAUTION! ONLY USE SPENT SHELLS. Once the shotshell has been fired, it's inert. Use a nail to drive the old primer back out of the base. Trim the plastic hull away, down to the base. Use a screw through the primer hole to attach the brass base to the wood. It's as easy as that.

Spent (used, fired) shotgun hulls make cool drawer pulls. "High brass" hulls work better.

Drawer pulls can be made from antler pieces by embedding knurled machine nuts in epoxy.

Drawer Pulls from Wood

When you start making furniture that has doors or drawers, you're going to need drawer handles or pulls. While deer antlers and shotshells look cool, bits of branches or logs also look great and are easier to make. It's a situation like this where crooked branches lend themselves well to making a good handle.

Natural wood can make interesting and useful pull handles.

Leveling a Four-Legged Piece

While using a grinder to level a slightly wobbly table or bench has already been covered, there is another way to correct a leg that is too long.

Place the piece upright on your workbench. Two of the legs touch all of the time, two don't touch unless you rock the piece back and forth. In most instances, one of the legs that touch all of the time is too long. Pull the table over to the edge of the workbench so that one of the long legs is hanging over the edge.

Check the tabletop with a level, then turn the table around and check it with a level with the other long leg off the table. Decide which way is most level.

As the piece sits with the longest leg hanging off the table, mark the leg for cutting, or use a Japanese saw to cut it in place, using the workbench top as a guide for the saw flats. Once the section is cut off, the table should be very close to being not wobbly. A little grinding with a rasp may take care of the final adjustment.

By sliding a Japanese saw along the surface of the workbench, this leg can be trimmed to the perfect length.

Log Accents

Adding log accents and features to existing furniture is a great way to bring a room together. It can be as complex as gluing on sheets of birch bark and patterns of twigs, or as easy as adding a few limbs.

If I do add limbs to a piece, I try to make it look like it belongs there and isn't something I just threw together. I like to use smaller logs or limbs as struts, gussets, columns, and trim. Even if they don't truly add structural strength to the piece, they do in appearance.

Adding arched branches to this piece adds strength to this piece visually and structurally.

139

Cutting Corner Logs

Some furniture designs require logs to act as trim to cover the corner edges. These logs require a special series of cuts to remove a ninety-degree section.

This work can be done on a table saw, but a jig to cradle the log securely is required. This process will require some math and critical thinking. In reality, it is less complex than it first appears.

The process is to take a log and secure it in a square cradle so that it can be safely and precisely cut while being held against the saw fence. Wood screws hold the log from two sides, allowing cuts to be made on the other two sides.

The cradle needs to be deep enough to hold the log, but shallow enough that the saw blade can reach the target depth. The cradle also needs to be long enough to allow all of the log to fit inside (Figure 1).

Most home table saws use 10" (250 mm) blades. While that sounds large, in most cases the blade only extends from the table about 3" (75 mm) when adjusted to its full height.

The jig will require four boards to make the U-shaped cradle. During the first cut, three boards are used. For the next cut, one side of the U will be removed, the cradle will be turned, and the remaining board attached to make another U.

In the example shown, boards Two and Four are 5½" (140 mm) wide, and boards One and Three are 4½" (114 mm) wide. I have marked them with numbers to show the process.

The first step in making the cradle is to screw board Two to the edges of boards One and Three to make a U. Place the log into the cradle and use a few screws to hold it in place on the top (board Two) and one side (board Three). No screws attach the log to board One. The log needs to be tight against the boards it is screwed to. The screw placement is critical, as it keeps the log from moving as it is cut (Figure 2).

A special-cut log works well to cover the corner of this chest of drawers. Notice how scraps of cedar cover the drawer fronts.

While the corner log covers the furniture joint, the scrap piece was used to hide the base.

Figure 1

Figure 2

Please note that the screws need to be short enough that the saw blade will not make contact with them, yet long enough to hold the log securely. In the example shown, 2" (50 mm) screws are used and driven into the log and cradle to the point that the heads are flush with the board surface. Since the cradle boards are ¾" (19 mm) thick, just over 1" (25 mm) of the screw is embedded into the log, which grabs it securely.

Once the log is secure, decide how deep of a cut is needed. Cutting to the center of the log is common. In the example shown, the black X is the middle (Figure 3).

The saw blade height is adjusted to the depth required for the cut. In the example shown, the blade was extended 2⅝" (67 mm) (Figures 4 and 5).

The second setting is the width of the cut, which includes the cradle board. In the example, the saw fence was set to 2⅝" (67 mm). Adding the width of the blade, the total width was 2¾" (70 mm) (Figures 6 and 7).

At these measurements, the blade will never contact the screws holding the logs (Figure 8).

Figure 3

Figure 4

Figure 5

Figure 6

Figure 7

Figure 8

After making the cut, leave the log in the cradle, but remove board One. Turn the cradle on its side and screw on board Four to the side of board Three (Figure 9).

The depth of the cut required measures 2 ⅞" (73 mm). The width of the cut requires the fence to be set at 3 ¼" (83 mm) (Figures 10 and 11).

Make the cut, but be careful that the saw blade doesn't kick the loose quarter of the log back when it falls free (Figure 12).

Remove the screws that secure the log to the cradle, and the corner log is complete (Figures 13 and 14).

While the setup sounds complex and bewildering, it becomes very simple as you gain experience.

Figure 9

Figure 10

Figure 11

Figure 12

Figure 13

Figure 14

These corner logs are posts of an entertainment center.

The screw holes are lost in the pattern of the hickory bark and will be even more once the log is sanded.

By rushing the process, the builder of this piece failed to smooth the wood surface, and also allowed paint chips and dirt to fall into the wet finish.

Quality and Workmanship

143

Rustic doesn't mean poor quality. I have seen pieces that have been thrown together and not sanded properly, joined properly, or finished well.

Case in point: A local gentlemen built a great deal of furniture and was trying to sell it during a local festival. From a distance the pieces looked great, but up close they looked awful. While he had done a great deal of work, the finish coats must have been done during a tornado. Bits of dirt, insects, and plant matter were stuck in the surface. I felt bad for him as customer after customer walked off shaking their heads.

Keep in mind that pieces need to be pleasing to the eye as well as the body. Splinters and rough surfaces can hurt.

Do the work required for a good job and you'll be making family heirlooms that will be handed down for generations. And that's a legacy anyone would love to have.

CHAPTER 29
MAKING MONEY
FROM SCRAPS

A byproduct of woodworking is scraps, and lots of them. Some are bland and get thrown into the fireplace. Others are too cool to burn. I save them for log furniture accessories and accents. What do I mean? I'm glad you asked. Nothing sets off a table, mantle, bookshelf, etc,, like a log candleholder or even a grouping of them. Are you having company over for drinks? No problem, just place log slice drink coasters around. The possibilities are endless.

Here are a few ideas.

Coasters

This is about as easy as it gets. Place a stop on your saw at ¾" (20 mm). Trim the log with the first cut to make sure the end is square. Hold the log against the stop and make a cut. The result should be a waferlike section of log ¾" (20 mm) thick.

If the raw coaster looks like the thickness you want, make successive cuts until you have the number of coasters desired. Bevel the edges of each coaster. Sand the sides and surfaces.

Coat with your choice of finishes.

Clamping a stop to the saw assures that each slice is the same thickness.

Coasters can save a tabletop from rings made by heat or water.

Tea Light Candleholder

The tea lights and LED versions now available fit into a 1½" (38 mm) hole.

To make a tea light candleholder, find a piece of log 3" (75 mm) in diameter or larger and cut it to the length you desire. I prefer 3" (75 mm) to 8" (200 mm) long.

Place the log section into the drill press vertically and drill a 1½" (38 mm) hole about ½" (13 mm) deep. Check the hole to make sure the candle or LED light will fit properly. Some tea lights are taller than others, so the hole may need to be deeper to achieve the desired look.

Bevel the edges and sand the entire piece to knock off any rough areas and highlight to bark and knots.

Coat it with your favorite finish.

145

Place the log upright in the drill press to assure that the hole will be perpendicular.

Tea light holders look great as a centerpiece on a table.

Candlestick Holder

You can make a single candlestick holder following the directions for the tea light holder, but make the hole 7⁄8" (22 mm) in diameter and about an inch (25 mm) deep.

If you would prefer a different look, lay the log section on its side and run it through a jointer or belt sander to flatten the bottom area. This keeps the candleholder from rolling over. Find the center of the top of the log and drill a 7⁄8" (22 mm) hole about an inch (25 mm) deep. If you want a grouping of candles, space more holes evenly across the log. Use a drill press to make sure the candles will be perfectly vertical.

Sand or plane the bottom of the log to make it flat.

The flat bottom keeps the candleholder from tipping over.

Space the holes evenly and in line.

Nothing is as beautiful as dinner by candlelight.

Logs naturally match dry floral arrangements.

Dry Arrangement Stand

Faux flower and seasonal arrangements can really brighten up a room and usher in the seasons. Placing them in a log or rustic holder only adds to the décor.

Making a stand is relatively simple. I prefer using a larger, heavier section of the log to prevent a gust of wind from blowing the display over.

Choose a log about 5" (125 mm) to 6" (150 mm) in diameter at the base. Trim it to about 8" (200 mm) to 10" (250 mm) tall.

Place the log section upright in the drill press and drill a hole about 1½" (40 mm) in diameter and 3" (75 mm), or more, deep.

Bevel the edges and sand the entire log to remove any rough spots. Coat with your choice of finish.

Napkin Rings

Placing a stop on your saw bed will assure that the slices are all the same thickness.

Use a wood clamp to hold the small sections of wood.

Log décor can extend to the dining area. Along with the candleholders and floral arrangement holder already listed, napkin rings are fairly simple to make.

Choose a log piece about 2½" (60 mm) to 3" (75 mm) in diameter. Trim the end to make it square and fresh.

Place a stop on your saw at 1½" (40 mm). This is to keep the rings the same thickness. The standard size of napkin rings is 1½" (40 mm) long with a 1½" (40 mm) hole.

Cut as many sections as you desire. A standard set is four to six rings.

Using a wood clamp to hold the rings, drill a 1½" (40 mm) hole through the center of the ring.

Bevel all edges, including the inside edges. Sand all surfaces, including the interior of the ring, to remove rough spots.

Coat with your finish of choice.

Log napkin rings bring a simple elegance to dinner.

RECOMMENDED READING

Rustic Artistry for the Home by Ralph Kylloe
ISBN: 978-0879059668

Understanding Wood: A Craftsman's Guide to Wood Technology
by R. Bruce Hoadley
ISBN: 978-1561583584

Understanding Wood Finishing by Bob Flexner
ISBN: 978-1565235663

Tree Craft: 35 Rustic Wood Projects That Bring the Outdoors In
by Chris Lubkemann
ISBN: 978-1565234550

Rustic Furniture Workshop by Daniel Mack
ISBN: 978-1579902209

Build Your Own Log Furniture: Ten Great Projects You Can Build for Fun or Profit by Les Smith and Dan Swesey
ISBN: 978-0970704603

A Reverence for Wood by Eric Sloane
ISBN: 978-0486433943

The Foxfire series of books by Eliot Wigginton
This is a 12-volume series starting with *The Foxfire Book.*

GLOSSARY

Antler rub – The damage caused when a male deer or elk rubs his antlers on a tree.

Bed post – The vertical members of a headboard or footboard for a bed frame.

Book sawn – The resulting color and grain matching wood created when cutting a log or board in two and used side by side like pages in a book.

Borate – A chemical used to treat wood to prevent rot and insect infestation.

Bucking – The process of removing branches from a log or sapling.

CA – Known officially as cyanoacrylate and unofficially as "super glue"; most woodworkers refer to it as CA.

Checking – A crack that runs the length of the log.

Coppicing – This is a practice in which hardwood trees are cut or pruned back to ground level, causing new, vigorous growth to sprout up.

Crotch – A place where a tree divides into two or more separate trunks.

Flitch – A longitudinal piece of wood cut from a tree with both live edges present.

Hardwood – Wood from a tree that bears leaves. (Oak, hickory, aspen, ash, etc.) This does not reference the density of the wood.

Heartwood – The central, non-living wood in a log. Generally is dense and of a deeper color than sapwood.

HVLP – High Volume Low Pressure. Used to describe the capabilities of a professional paint or finish sprayer.

Japanese saw – (Nokogiri) A saw that originated in Japanese woodworking that cuts on the pull stroke and has no kerf.

Kiln – A device used to dry wood.

Lacquer – A clear, fast-drying, solvent-based finish for wood.

Live edge – The portion of a board or slab that used to be the exposed face of the tree.

Moisture content – The amount of moisture in wood, measured as a percentage.

Mortise – The female section of a joint that is cut to accept a matching tenon.

Native lumber – Unfinished lumber made from locally cut wood.

Polyurethane – A polymer-based finish for wood.

Punk – Wood that is soft from the onset of rot.

Quartersawn – The technique of sawing boards so that the annual rings are at a right angle to the board face.

Bed rails – The horizontal members in a headboard or footboard. This can also refer to the sideboards that connect the headboard and footboard.

Sapling – A young tree not over four inches in diameter.

Sapwood – The newer, living wood that carries water and nutrients in a tree. Is generally pale and less dense than the heartwood.

Sawbuck – A cradle to hold logs while being worked upon.

Shoots – Rapid new growth that is commonly found on the stumps of freshly cut trees.

Slab – In general, a slab is a thick section of wood. It can have cut edges, live edges, or both.

Softwood – Wood from trees that bear needles (pine, fir, spruce, cedar).

Spalting – Caused by fungi in wood. It commonly leaves intricate black lines and is highly sought after by woodworkers.

Steam bending – The process of heating wood with steam to make it pliable.

Swiss work – A technique used to decorate the surface of a piece of furniture with straight twigs laid side by side in corduroy fashion.

Tenon – The male section of a joint that is shaped to fit into a matching hole known as a mortise.

Urethane glue – A strong, water-proof foaming glue that fills voids in joints.

Waney edge – The portion of a board or slab that used to be the exposed face of the tree.

Warping – The twisting and or bending of wood caused by uneven drying of the wood or natural strain in the wood.

149

INDEX

ABOUT THE AUTHOR

Alan J. Garbers started woodworking when he was just a small lad growing up in Minnesota. Alan is now an award-winning outdoor writer, author, and photographer. Along with woodworking, he enjoys fishing, hunting, hiking, canoeing, photography, writing, cowboy action shooting, and more.

Alan loves exploring the BWCAW in northern Minnesota, roaming the deserts of Arizona, or Jeeping the mountains of Colorado. He has lived in Minnesota, Hawaii, Mississippi, Florida, Colorado, Arizona, and Indiana. From hunting rattlesnakes to black bear and fishing for catfish to muskie, he loves it all.

His writing credits have included hundreds of articles in *Indiana Outdoor News, Indiana Game & Fish, Muzzle Blasts, Outdoor Guide Magazine, Fur-Fish-Game, Boundary Waters Journal, Boys' Quest, Fun for Kidz, Mother Earth News, Cricket, Small Farm Today, American Careers, Arizona Hunter & Angler, Old West, Woodcarving Illustrated*, and others.

Topics range from turkey and deer hunting to crappie and bass fishing, from snorkeling in the tropics to making maple syrup in Indiana.

Fiction credits include *Star Trek: Strange New Worlds* anthologies IV, V, and VIII.

In 2012, Alan compiled an anthology from his popular monthly column, *Behind the Badge: True Stories of Indiana's Conservation Officers*. It is available in e-reader format and found at Amazon and other on-line book retailers.

PHOTO CREDITS

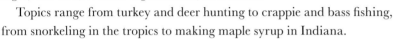